Scottish Official Publications:

an introduction and guide

By John Moore & Kay Munro

the Stationery Office

HOLYROOD

Applications for reproduction should be made in writing to The Stationery Office Limited, St Crispins, Duke Street, Norwich NR3 1PD.

The information contained in the publication is believed to be correct at time of manufacture. Whilst care has been taken to ensure that the information is accurate, the publisher can accept no responsibility for any errors or omissions or for changes to the details given.

A CIP catalogue record for this book is available from the British Library.
A Library of Congress CIP catalogue record has been applied for

First published 2001
ISBN 0 11 4972915

A Note from the Sponsor

Holyrood Magazine began life shortly after the Scotland Bill became the Scotland Act. Over the months it has grown and evolved alongside the Scottish Parliament and has established itself as a key forum for information, analysis and debate on the issues affecting MSPs and the people they have been elected to serve.

The magazine is read by Members of the Scottish Parliament and their teams, by employees of the Parliament and Scottish Executive, MPs, MEPs and subscribers from across Scotland's key organisations, institutions and companies. We rely on, and would wish to acknowledge, the support and encouragement of our Editorial Board of MSPs, their colleagues, and the Presiding Officer, Clerk and staff of the Scottish Parliament.

Holyrood Magazine also owes a lot to those organisations with which we have developed alliances, across the public, voluntary and private sectors. Key amongst those working friendships is that with the Stationery Office which, in partnership with the Parliament, makes the proceedings in the Chamber and Committees available for scrutiny by those in the outside world.

The open parliament envisaged by those who campaigned for a Scottish Parliament and then drew up the procedures to run it has, to a great extent, been achieved. That open parliament relies on information being made available – though few could have predicted quite how much information would be generated and how many sources would be open to the researcher. Westminster and the European Institutions too have made remarkable strides in this respect. This book sets out to steer those seeking information on subjects to the right places. *Holyrood Magazine* is delighted and honoured to be associated with this guide.

John Macgill
Editorial Director
Holyrood Magazine

Contents

Acknowledgements

Any published work is a corporate effort and there are many to whom we are indebted. In particular, we must record our admiration and sincere thanks to the staff responsible for the various web-sites listed in this book. We would also like to thank a number of individuals - these are, in Glasgow, Andrew Wale, Director of Library Services, and our colleagues, William Nixon and Kirsteen McKenna, all at Glasgow University Library and, in Edinburgh, Fiona Myles at Edinburgh Central Library, Jane McNair at TSO and the publishers of Holyrood Magazine who have generously sponsored the publication.

Foreword

By Professor Sir Neil MacCormick MEP

In the contemporary European Union, there is concern about respect for subsidiarity. Is too much being done too centrally? There is parallel concern about a deficit in democratic controls. On the one hand, electoral turn-out for European parliamentary elections tends to be low in all member states relatively to parliamentary elections at the level of the state or its internal nations and regions. Turnout has been declining election-by-election since the introduction of direct elections to the European Parliament. The Irish Referendum on Nice has given out another danger signal about detachedness from the Union among the citizen body.

Again, there is an ever-increasing volume of law and regulation that has its origin at Union level, and this has reduced the real scope for law making in what remain at least in theory sovereign legislative bodies of the member states. Member State Parliaments may find themselves obliged to transpose large bodies of law that their members were unaware of during the European legislative process, and of which they may not approve, while their legislative discretion in other domains is limited by the obligation to respect the community *acquis*.

This relative diminution in power of Member State Parliaments is at its most alarming in those areas which are subject to qualified majority voting in the Council of Ministers, but not to co-decision with the European Parliament. Democratic self-government requires legislative decision-making to take place in public after public deliberation by elected legislators. The Executive branch of government has properly the role of preparing legislative programmes and bringing these before the legislature for its consideration and for rejection or adoption by it, with or without amendment.

In the domains which are now subject to decision by the intergovernmental method in the Union's second and third pillars (and even on crucial matters including agriculture and fisheries in the first pillar), legislative democracy is severely compromised. Members of the Executive Branch of the several states deliberating in secret become the effective legislature for the Union, without adequate answerability either to the Parliaments of the member states or to the European Parliament.

Even where co-decision prevails, deliberation in the Council proceeds in secret, so that the Executive government of each Member State makes its own input to the community legislative process in a way that precludes real answerability to the domestic legislature. The power (often in practice no more than a theoretical power) to dismiss a government after the event is no substitute for the power to control or at least influence the process of law making in its detail during the law-making process.

In several member states federal and quasi-federal forms of government exist that allocate to regions or nations internal to the state legislative and executive power in relation to important domains, such as home affairs and justice, education and research, cultural affairs, industrial development, and internal transport. It is extremely important to ensure that there are clear lines of communication in both directions connecting legislatures at this level to the Union legislative process in a way that makes possible prior scrutiny of and comment upon legislative proposals at sufficiently early stage in the process. It is no less true of these legislatures that they are bound by the *acquis communautaire,* and that in many domains their legislative activities are affected by the obligation to transpose relevant Directives in a locally appropriate way.

Considerations such as the above indicate what a vitally important function the present book serves, and how vital is the collaboration among Scottish University library and information services from which it emerges. The best answer to a democracy deficit in the European Union is to do something about the information deficit. People in general and people with professional, commercial, or employment-based concerns about governance in Europe and about the quality of the legal and regulatory environment in which we live, move and have our being, need as much and as clear information as possible about all the parliaments and executive bodies that contribute to the overall frame of government.

It is a curious fact that attention to subsidiarity increases complexity. The principle of subsidiarity recommends that all governmental tasks be carried out at a level as close to the citizens affected as is consistent with equity and with efficiency in the pursuit of common goods. This implies that, for example, environmental legislation needs at least a European if not also a global reach in the setting of common standards. But the local and detailed elaboration and application of these common standards needs sensitivity, well-measured discretion, and a great deal of local knowledge if the overall scheme is actually to achieve its objectives. We are therefore fated to live with multiple levels of government, and we certainly have a multiplicity of levels in the Scotland of today.

Therefore we need thoroughly efficient information systems that enable us to cope with complexity by finding our way through the regulatory maze in a way that connects citizen understanding with legislative and executive action. The present volume makes a highly effective and thus extremely welcome contribution to this end.

I have one regret about chapter 5. There is an admirable section about the information offices of the European Parliament as an institution, and these offices, not least the Scottish office run by Mr Dermot Scott and his team, do a splendid job. But Parliaments, it must be remembered, are above all representative institutions that have to take part in making the laws and in keeping executive government effectively answerable to citizens. So the other point of contact that all citizens, even academics and professionals in their academic/professional capacity, have to have is with their own elected representatives.

There are eight representatives of Scotland in the European Parliament. Since 1999, they represent Scotland in a very particular sense. For all are MEPs for Scotland. Under the list system of proportional representation introduced to elections from the UK to the European Parliament in 1999, Scotland is a single constituency with eight representatives (three Labour, two Scottish National Party, two Conservatives, one Liberal democrat). For some purposes, we pursue vigorous intellectual and political combat with each other as mandated by the principles of the parties whose voters elected us. For others, where there is a common view of a common and legitimate Scottish interest, we pull together as a highly effective team.

This is another aspect of subsidiarity, involving an interaction between representatives in government between different levels. Since this is also of importance in the mutual-information process, I would add to the information sources available the following eight e-mail addresses:
eattwooll@europarl.eu.int ihudghton@europarl.eu.int
nmaccormick@europarl.eu.int dwmartin@europarl.eu.int bmiller@europarl.eu.int
jpurvis@europarl.eu.int sstevenson@europarl.eu.int cstihler@europarl.eu.int

Having an academic role, relevant to this preface, as well as the role of one of the two SNP MEPs, it would be out of place to argue here for the proposal my party would make about simplifying levels of governance, by squeezing out the intermediate Westminster tier. But let me simply mention it as an index to the fact that there genuinely are points of difference as well as of agreement among the Scottish eight. Seek information from us too, but seek it widely!

Introduction

Background

'There shall be a Scottish Parliament'

When First Minister, Donald Dewar used the opening words of the Scotland Act in his speech at the State Opening of Parliament, he underlined the reality of devolved government for Scotland. Taken in a longer perspective, the establishment of the new Scottish Parliament in 1999 was only part of a series of steps in an extended process of devolved government in the United Kingdom. In the late 1960s, a House of Commons Scottish Affairs Select Committee was first appointed and this became a permanent feature of the departmental committee system in 1979. Scottish ministers also had their own regular Question Time in the House of Commons. Other changes aimed to improve the handling of specifically Scottish matters at Westminster without recourse to a separate Parliament. As an example of this, the Scottish Grand Committee's remit and powers were expanded in the mid-1990s and it was able to meet outside of Westminster and Edinburgh.

After the 1997 general election, the Labour government arranged for a referendum on the proposals set out in the White Paper, **'Scotland's Parliament'** (http://www.scotland.gov.uk/government/devolution/scpa-00.asp). The referendum was held on 11 September 1997 and produced clear majorities for the two propositions about the creation of a Scottish Parliament and its having certain tax-varying powers. Following this, the Scotland Bill was introduced in January 1998 and resulted in the Scotland Act in November that year. As part of the process, the Secretary of State for Scotland appointed a Consultative Steering Group to recommend proposals for the practical operation of the new Parliament. After a period of detailed consultation, its report, **Shaping Scotland's Parliament** (http://www.scotland.gov.uk/library/documents-w5/rcsg-00.htm), was used as the blueprint for the Parliament's initial set of Standing Orders. The new Parliament began sitting in May 1999 and those powers, which were to be its responsibility, were formally transferred.

The devolution settlement means that the Scottish Parliament has 'devolved' powers within the United Kingdom. Any powers remaining with the UK Parliament at Westminster are 'reserved'. However, the Scottish Parliament operates as a Parliament in its own right. Legislation can be passed by it without going through Westminster and, while the UK Parliament retains power to legislate on any matter, the convention of devolution is that it will not normally legislate on devolved matters without the consent of the Scottish Parliament. To clarify the division of matters, the Scottish Parliament and Executive have responsibility for these specific devolved areas of legislation:

▶ **The arts**

▶ **Economic development**

▶ **Education and training**

▶ **The environment**

▶ **Farming, fishing and forestry**

▶ **Health**

▶ **Housing**

▶ **Law and order (the police, the courts and lawyers)**

▶ **Local government**

▶ **Social work services**

▶ **Sport**

▶ **Transport**

The Scottish Parliament can also vary taxation by up to 3p in the pound.

Reserved matters dealt with by the UK Parliament at Westminster include:

▶ **Constitutional issues**

▶ **Defence**

▶ **Employment**

▶ **Foreign policy, including the European Union**

▶ **Immigration and nationality**

▶ **Social security benefits**

▶ **Telecommunications**

Following the implementation of devolution, Scotland's role at Westminster is changing. The role of Scottish MPs and Ministers will reflect the existence and activities of the Scottish Parliament, while Westminster business and practices will also adjust to reflect the changes in Scotland and in other parts of the UK. These changes will have an impact on all aspects of government in the United Kingdom – in particular, the Scotland Act provided for a reduction in the number of Scottish seats in the

Westminster Parliament. Despite this prospect of change, we, as authors, believe that there is a need for a guide to the official publications of the various levels of government in Scotland.

Official Publications is an area of information provision well known for its complexity and its confusing jargon. All too often, people seeking information from official sources are thwarted because of the terminology or an inexact sense of the responsibilities of various levels of government. There are many published guides and bibliographies which seek to aid the user through what can be a difficult field but it is also true that many works can be equally confusing by their depth of detail. In a time of growing use and reliance on the Internet as the prime source for information, a complex situation can become even more confusing.

This guide has developed from our experience in dealing with this new pattern of publishing, in answering a wide range of enquiries relating to all aspects of official publications and in running training courses for professional colleagues. Our intention has been to provide a tool for the hard-pressed individual who wants a relatively quick and straightforward introduction to the most useful sources and documents in what is a very wide range of available material. Both paper and electronic formats are discussed and we have attempted to set the publications in context. The book is not intended to be a comprehensive and analytical consideration of every issue relating to the publication of official documents in Scotland.

Inevitably, this book will become dated quickly because of the increasing rate of change in electronic provision. The re-designing and alteration of familiar web-addresses and search engines, which are frequently unannounced, seem to be part of contemporary information provision. Sites will change and should become easier to use, search engines will become more refined than the rather blunt instruments they are at present and, because of this, we have tried to avoid any criticism or evaluation of the web-sites discussed. Nonetheless, we believe that the book will have a value in bringing together many of the disparate strands in official publishing. Given this climate of change, we recommend that readers consult the **United Kingdom Official Publications Collection web-site** (http://www.lib.gla.ac.uk/Depts/MOPS/Offpub/index.html) at Glasgow University Library for the most recent addresses of all the web-sites discussed in this book.

In trying to bring together an extensive range of descriptions of processes and publications, we are greatly aware of the work done by the information staff in many Parliamentary and government bodies and we wish to record our indebtedness to them.

John Moore and Kay Munro
6 July 2001

Official Publications from the Scottish Parliament

Chapter 1

The Scottish Parliament

I n this chapter, we consider the printed and electronic publications emanating from the contemporary Scottish Parliament, along with some other relevant background material. As most users will be aware, Scotland had a separate Parliament prior to the Act of Union in 1707. The Acts of this Parliament (1124-1707) were gathered and edited, under the direction of the Commissioners on the Public Records, by Thomas Thomson and Cosmo Innes in thirteen volumes between 1814-1875. The volumes also cover certain other parliamentary proceedings and are written in Scots. Some Scots Acts are still in force. More detailed information on the pre-1707 Parliament can be found on the **Scottish Parliament Project web-site** based at the University of St. Andrews (http://www.st-and.ac.uk/~scotparl/index.htm).

One of the most immediate results of devolution in Scotland was a marked increase in the publication of official material relating to governance and legislation. The creation of the new Parliament provided an opportunity to establish new methods of practice. An initial major concern was the development of an effective information strategy. The report of the Consultative Steering Group highlighted the basic objective in the belief that:

> 'Only well-informed citizens can maximise the opportunities which this [an open, accessible and participative Information Service] presents for individuals and organisations to contribute to the democratic process. Only well-informed MSPs can contribute fully to the governance of Scotland'. (*Report of the Consultative Steering Group on the Scottish Parliament,* 1998. p.142).

Much consideration and debate has been given to the creation of both external and internal information services, in particular that information about the Parliament should be available equally to all parts of society. Expert advice recommended the use of new technology to ensure an effective flow of information. With this in mind, the **Parliament web-site** (http://www.scottish. parliament.uk/) was created and this is the primary source for information for all proceedings and papers of the Scottish Parliament.

As an additional element in this strategy, the Scottish Parliament Public Information Service was established to facilitate the answering of enquiries and provide details about the Parliament and its business. To assist information access at a local level, Partner Libraries have been identified in each constituency and links have been created with the Information Centre. In all, there are seventy-six public libraries acting as Partner Libraries, providing focal points in the local community with access to comprehensive information, in printed and electronic format, from and about the Parliament. Partner Libraries do vary in what publications they hold and a list of these libraries can be found at http://www.scottish.parliament.uk/msps/partnerlib.htm.

It is important to point out that the current pattern of publishing in both formats is still quite fluid and there has been noticeable change already in the production and publishing of material. While the rapidity of change is likely to decline, this pattern of dynamism will continue.

In truth, there is a vast amount of information available about the Parliament and its activities. Much is available both in printed and electronic format. Everything published by the Scottish Parliament is available on their web-site. However, there are several publications that never appear in printed format but are only available electronically. A further important point to remember is that publications are numbered according to Session (i.e. the length of a Parliament) and not year. A session normally lasts for four years. In other words, Session 1 publications cover the first Parliament from the date of the first meeting following the Scottish parliamentary election in 1999 until its dissolution in 2003. Sessions are divided into Parliamentary years for the purpose of arranging business. The first Parliamentary year is the year beginning with the date of the first meeting of the Parliament following a Scottish parliamentary election.

It can be confusing to the occasional user, particularly those who are uncertain about the responsibilities of different tiers of government. In addition, the individual documents presented before Parliament, such as Bills, Motions and Petitions, can appear in several different publications and formats. Apart from the inevitable skill problems imposed on the individual user by an emphasis on the electronic format, certain elements of the information strategy can be mutually exclusive and several aspects of the service are duplicated. Nevertheless, the staff of various offices of the Parliament must be commended for the level of detail and width of information coverage they provide. Given this range of material and its complexity, we have tried to avoid an over-elaboration of the detailed descriptions provided by the Information Service itself and have sought to direct readers to these comprehensive sources, where available.

Scottish Parliament Web-site

(http://www.scottish.parliament.uk/)

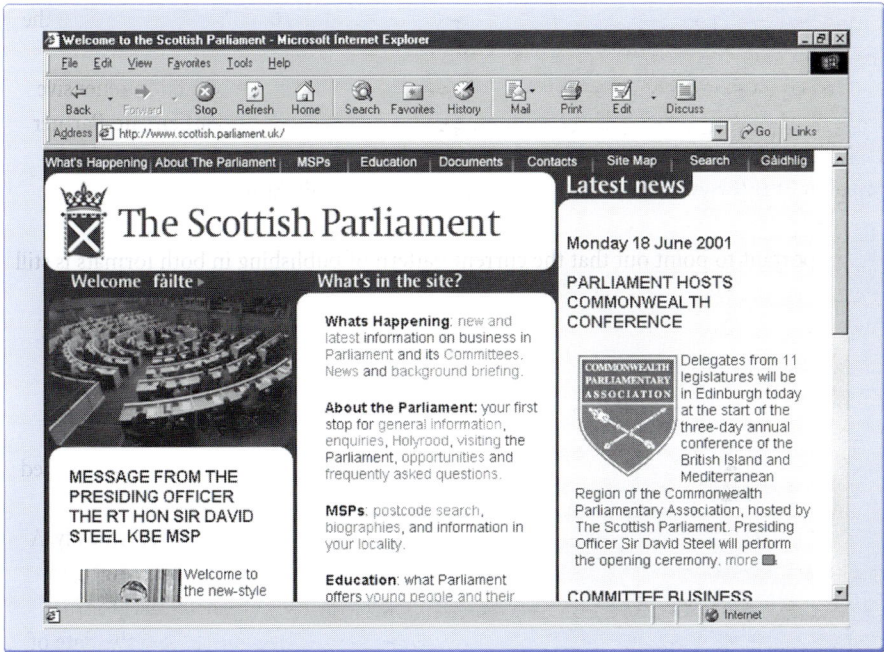

This is a large and complex web-site. Many pages appear to be similar but frequently contain different information. It can be difficult for users to know what section of the web-site they are in and, to aid navigation of the site, users should note that a horizontal bar appears under the section of the web-site currently being viewed.

The site is currently divided into five principal sections plus a **contacts page** (http://www.scottish.parliament.uk/contact.html) which can be accessed from the tool bar along the top of the webpage or under the 'What's in the site?' section. A major element of the home page is a 'Latest News' column which includes news information on Committee business (e.g. dates and locations of meetings, witnesses called to give evidence). A brief description of the contents of the five principal sections is listed below:

▶ **What's Happening** (http://www.scottish.parliament.uk/whats_happening/ wh.html) – daily information on Parlimentary and Committee business. Events due to be webcast are identified, as are items posted that day. The page is divided into two main columns - a 'Timetable' column which lists Parliamentary business for that week and includes links to forthcoming Committee agendas and papers.

This column is headed by links to a news release providing an 'at a glance guide' to the week ahead in the Scottish Parliament and to the current Business Bulletin. The 'Latest' column contains information on what has been published by Parliament in the last few days, including news releases, Official Reports, Scottish Parliament Papers and research publications. Each item is hypertext linked and will take you to the electronic version of the document. At the left-hand side of the page there is a column of hypertext links to key areas of the Scottish Parliament web-site including Business Bulletins, Committees, Meetings of the Parliament, Bills, Written Answers and WHISP (see below).

▶ **About the Parliament** (http://www.scottish.parliament.uk/welcoming_you/ wy.html) - this part of the site is about visiting and contacting the Parliament, its history and how it works. It also includes information on both the temporary home of the Parliament and the new building currently being constructed on the Holyrood site,

▶ **MSPs** (http://www.scottish.parliament.uk/msps/msps.html) –contains information on Members of the Scottish Parliament (MSPs), including background biography, contact details, **register of interests** (http://www.scottish.parliament.uk/msps/ interests/register-00.htm), and parliamentary activities (e.g. membership of committees, cross party groups, posts held),

▶ **Education** (http://www.scottish.parliament.uk/ypt/ypt.html) - developed by the Education Service of the Scottish Parliament to provide a range of resources and services for young people, teachers and others interested in learning about the Parliament,

▶ **Documents** (http://www.scottish.parliament.uk/parl_bus/pab.html) - this section brings together the complete runs of all parliamentary publications, including educational resources and factfiles.

There are also links to:
▶ **Search** (http://www.scottish.parliament.uk/search.html) - the Parliament's search engine (see below),

▶ **Site map** (http://www.scottish.parliament.uk/sitemap.htm) which provides a link to **Scottish Parliament Live** (http://www.scottishparliamentlive.com/), the Parliament's web-casting service,

▶ **Gaelic** (http://www.scottish.parliament.uk/gaidhlig/gaidhlig.htm) versions of the whole site.

Searching the Scottish Parliament Web-site
(http://www.scottish.parliament.uk/search.htm)

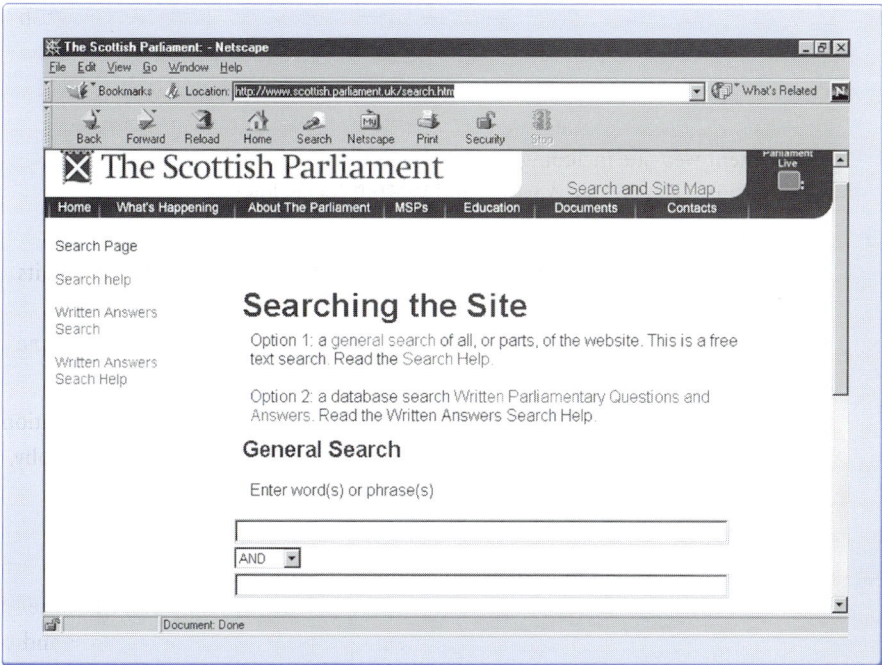

The Scottish Parliament: - Netscape
File Edit View Go Window Help
Bookmarks Location: http://www.scottish.parliament.uk/search.htm What's Related

Back Forward Reload Home Search Netscape Print Security Stop

The Scottish Parliament
Search and Site Map

Home | What's Happening | About The Parliament | MSPs | Education | Documents | Contacts

Search Page

Search help

Written Answers
Search

Written Answers
Seach Help

Searching the Site

Option 1: a general search of all, or parts, of the website. This is a free
text search. Read the Search Help.

Option 2: a database search Written Parliamentary Questions and
Answers. Read the Written Answers Search Help.

General Search

Enter word(s) or phrase(s)

AND

Document: Done

The search page provides users with two search options, both allowing Boolean and phrase searching:

▶ **Option 1**: a general search of all, or parts, of the web-site. There is an instructional guide to searching this site at http://www.scottish.parliament.uk/help.htm. As in all searching, it helps greatly if the user reads the help guide. The search engine allows free text searching across the whole site or specific areas (e.g. **Business Bulletin**) which can help limit and speed searches. A general search across the whole site can result in several hundred hits, not all of which may be relevant. However, a percentage rating is displayed alongside each hit - the higher this is, the greater the occurrence of the search term. Users should note that this does not necessarily mean a greater relevance and frequently a lower percentage rating is as valuable a hit. One significant point is that the search results do not highlight the search term(s). This is particularly relevant when searching for statistical information or the contribution of individual MSPs (e.g. a search in the Official Report under a surname will return results of their voting record as well as their contributions to debates.

▶ **Option 2**: a database search of Written Parliamentary Questions and Answers using the template provided and by entering search terms in one or more of the fields or selecting from the drop-down lists. There is also an instructional guide to searching parliamentary questions and answers at http://www.scottish.parliament.uk/help-pq.htm.

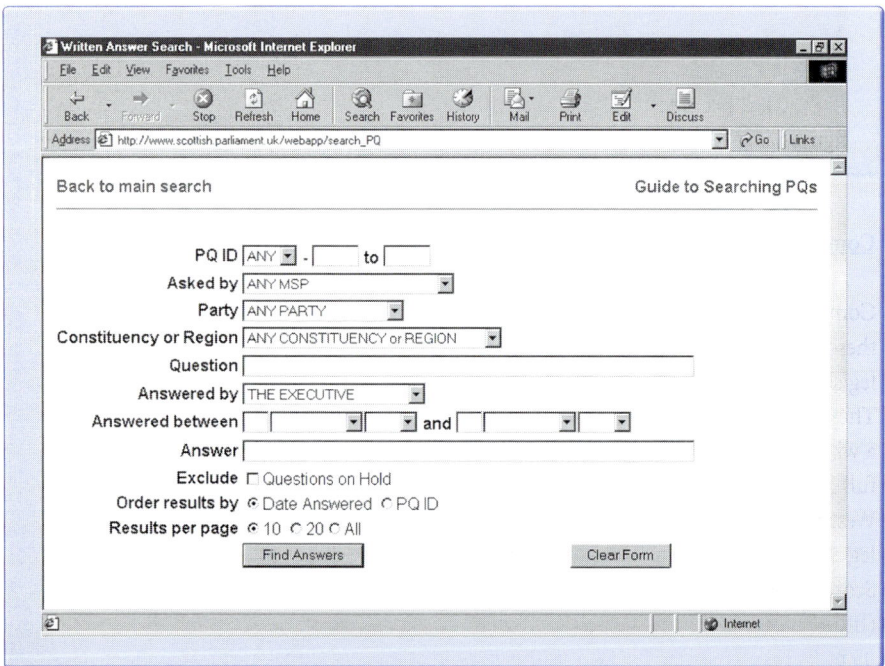

The Business of the Scottish Parliament

The ability of the Scottish Parliament to enact legislation on a considerable range of issues is a major distinguishing feature of devolved government in Scotland. The Parliament operates through full meetings of all Members and Committee meetings of smaller groups of between five and fifteen MSPs. Much of the business brought before Parliament is on behalf of the Scottish Executive and reflects the policies of the government of the day.

Parliament conducts its business according to certain rules called **Standing Orders** (http://www.scottish.parliament.uk/parl_bus/sto-c.htm). Users seeking more detailed information on a particular point of procedure should consult the **Parliamentary Procedure** section (http://www.scottish.parliament.uk/parl_bus/proced.html) of the Parliament web-site. The programme of business for Parliament is drawn up by the Parliamentary Bureau, a representative group of Members from the constituent political parties chaired by the Presiding Officer, giving consideration to deadlines, Bills and other concerns. For example, the Bureau ensures that time is allocated for Ministers to make statements to Parliament on matters of policy or legislation. The agreed programme and the daily business list are published in the **Business Bulletin**. The full Parliament does not meet when Committees are sitting (usually all day Tuesday and Wednesday morning).

A very useful brief guide to the Parliament can be found in **Factfile No. 3 How the Scottish Parliament Works** (http://www.scottish.parliament.uk/welcoming_you/ ff3.htm). It provides background to the establishment of the Parliament, the key figures, and its working practices.

Committees

Committees have considerable powers and can investigate issues within their remit - these are known as Competent Matters. These include legislative proposals, European legislation and the policy and administration of many aspects of Scottish government. They can initiate their own legislation through Committee Bills, call anyone to attend as a witness and meet jointly with other Committees. Their reports are presented to the full Parliament or to other Committees. A significant difference compared with the Westminster process is the leading role they have through the stages of consideration of legislative proposals. For more information on the functions of Committees in the Scottish Parliament, see the SPICe Subject Map on **Scottish Parliament Committees** (http://www.scottish.parliament.uk/whats_happening/research/pdf_subj_maps/smsp-05.pdf) or the relevant section of the guide by Jane Convery, entitled *The Governance of Scotland: a Saltire Guide* (2000). Certain Committees, such as European, are required by the Parliament's Standing Orders and are known as Mandatory Committees. Other Committees (Subject Committees) are established by Parliament to consider particular areas of public policy.

Presently, there are eighteen Committees, all of which produce an Official Report and Minutes of Proceedings for each meeting held. It should be pointed out that the Committee Minutes of Proceedings are not available separately in printed form but appear in the Committee Reports, which are published as SP Papers. The Minutes are available electronically Each Committee has an abbreviation which is used in the citation of publications. The current Committees of the Scottish Parliament, with their abbreviations and remits, are:

Audit Committee (AU) (http://www.scottish.parliament.uk/official_report/cttee/aud.htm) - to consider and report on upon any accounts or other documents laid before the Parliament concerning finances in relation to public expenditure, including reports by the Auditor General,

Education, Culture and Sport Committee (ED) (http://www.scottish.parliament.uk/ official_report/cttee/educ.htm) - to consider and report on school and pre-school education matters falling within the responsibility of the Minister for Education, Europe and External Affairs; and on matters relating to the arts, culture and sport within the responsibility of the Minister for Environment, Sport and Culture,

Enterprise and Lifelong Learning Committee (EL) (http://www.scottish.parliament.uk/ official_report/cttee/enter.htm) - to consider and report on issues relating to the Scottish economy, industry, tourism, training and further and higher education, and other matters within the remit of the Minister for Enterprise and Lifelong Learning,

Equal Opportunities Committee (EO) (http://www.scottish.parliament.uk/official_report/ cttee/equal.htm) - to consider and report on equal opportunities within the Parliament. This includes the prevention, elimination or regulation of discrimination between persons on grounds of sex or marital status, on racial grounds, or on grounds of disability, age, sexual orientation, language or social origin, or of other personal attributes, such as religious beliefs or political opinions,

European Committee (EU) (http://www.scottish.parliament.uk/official_report/cttee/ europe.htm) - to consider and report on proposals for, and the implementation of, European Communities legislation and any other European Union issue,

Finance Committee (FI) (http://www.scottish.parliament.uk/official_report/cttee/ finance.htm) - to consider and report on any documents laid before the Parliament by the Executive which contain proposals or budgets involving public expenditure or proposals for the making of a tax-varying resolution and on any Committee report setting out proposals concerning public expenditure. The Committee also considers Budget Bills and any matters relating to the expenditure of the Scottish Administration or other expenditure payable out of the Scottish Consolidated Fund. It may also consider and report to the Parliament on the timetable or the Stages of Budget Bills and on the handling of financial business,

Health and Community Care Committee (HE) (http://www.scottish.parliament.uk/ official_report/cttee/health.htm) - to consider and report on issues relating to the health policy and the National Health Service in Scotland and other matters within the responsibility of the Minister for Health and Community Care,

Justice 1 Committee (J1) (http://www.scottish.parliament.uk/official_report/cttee/ just1.htm) - to consider and report on matters relating to the administration of civil and criminal justice, the reform of the civil and criminal law and such other matters as fall within the responsibility of the Minister for Justice. Note that with effect from Jan 8th 2001 the **Justice 1 Committee** succeeded the **Justice and Home Affairs Committee (JH)**

Justice 2 Committee (J2) (http://www.scottish.parliament.uk/official_report/cttee/ just2.htm) – has the same remit as Justice 1 Committee,

Local Government Committee (LG) (http://www.scottish.parliament.uk/official_report/ cttee/local.htm) - to consider and report on local government matters falling within the responsibility of the Minister for Finance and Local Government,

Private Bills (http://www.scottish.parliament.uk/official_report/cttee/private.htm) - to consider and report on the Bill in question. Each Committee will be named after the Bill it is discussing and each Committee is normally established for the duration of the Bill,

Procedures Committee (PR) (http://www.scottish.parliament.uk/official_report/cttee/proced.htm) - to consider the practice and procedures of the Parliament in relation to its public business,

Public Petitions Committee (PE) (http://www.scottish.parliament.uk/official_report/cttee/petit.htm) - to consider and report on the admissibility of public petitions and what action is to be taken upon them,

Rural Development Committee (RD) (http://www.scottish.parliament.uk/official_report/cttee/rural.htm) - to consider and report on matters relating to rural development, agriculture and fisheries and related matters falling within the responsibility of the Minister for Rural Development. Note that with effect from Jan 8th 2001 the Rural Affairs Committee (RA) changed its title to **Rural Development Committee**,

Social Justice Committee (SJ)
(http://www.scottish.parliament.uk/official_report/cttee/social.htm) - to consider and report on matters relating to housing and the voluntary sector and related matters within the responsibility of the Minister for Social Justice. Note that with effect from Jan 8th 2001 the Social Inclusion, Housing and Voluntary Sector Committee (HS) changed its title to **Social Justice Committee**,

Standards Committee (ST) (http://www.scottish.parliament.uk/official_report/cttee/stan.htm) - to consider and report on matters relating to the conduct of members in carrying out their Parliamentary duties and the adoption, amendment and application of any Code of Conduct for Members,

Subordinate Legislation Committee (SL) (http://www.scottish.parliament.uk/official_report/cttee/subord.htm) - to consider and report on subordinate legislation laid before the Parliament. This includes any general Scottish Statutory Instrument not laid before the Parliament, proposed powers to make subordinate legislation in particular Bills or other proposed legislation, and all general questions relating to powers to make subordinate legislation,

Transport and Environment Committee (TE) (http://www.scottish.parliament.uk/official_report/cttee/trans.htm) - to consider and report on transport matters within the responsibility of the Minister for Transport, and matters relating to environment and natural heritage falling within the responsibility of the Minister for Environment, Sport and Culture.

Information on Committees is best accessed through the **Parliamentary Committees** (http://www.scottish.parliament.uk/official_report/cttee.html) section of the Parliament web-site. Here you will find links to the home pages of each Committee. Each home page lists the convenor, membership and remit of the Committee, as well as direct links to agendas and all reports and papers produced by them. Links to the Committees' **Official Report** and **Minutes of Proceedings** are also provided.

Both **WHISP** (http://www.scottish.parliament.uk/whats_happening/whisp.html) and the **Business Bulletin** (http://www.scottish.parliament.uk/agenda_and_decisions/forth.html) are also useful sources of information on Committee business including agendas of forthcoming meetings. **Committee news releases** (http://www.scottish.parliament.uk/whats_happening/new.html - comm) are another valuable source of information on Committee work.

The SPICe subject map **Scottish Parliament Committees** (http://www.scottish. parliament.uk/whats_happening/research/pdf_subj_maps/smsp-05.pdf) and **Factfile 3 How the Scottish Parliament Works** (http://www.scottish.parliament.uk/ welcoming_you/ff3.htm#comm) both provide a brief outline on the Committee system and their work.

MSPs

Although Parliamentary activity reflects the policies of the government of the day, the role of the individual MSP is very important in bringing matters of local and national importance before the whole Parliament. Individual Members can raise issues before Parliament by asking Oral Questions, submitting Written Questions or moving a Motion. At the end of a meeting of Parliament, there is an allocated period of 30 minutes (Decision Time) when Parliament votes on the questions before it that day. Following that time, Members may raise items of business under Members' Business (usually debating the subject of Motions).

The Legislative Process

Bills

A major function of Parliament is to consider and debate proposed legislation, usually as submissions in the form of Bills. Most Bills are presented on behalf of the Executive or a Committee but individual Members can introduce their own Bills, if supported by eleven other Members. Executive Bills are **not** the first stage in the process – usually public consultation has taken place before they are presented (see Chapter 2). A distinctive feature of Scottish Parliament Bills is that they retain their original numbering throughout their passage. The printed version of a Bill appears on purple-tinted paper with a running number, regardless of type (e.g. SP Bill 4). On the back page of the printed Bill is its title, long title, the Member introducing it, the date of introduction, its supporters and its type. At this time, additional papers are published (on white paper) to accompany the Bill. These are:

a)   **Explanatory Notes** (e.g. SP Bill 4-EN), which provide an explanation to the Bill and also include a financial memorandum detailing costs which would be met by either the Executive, local authorities or other bodies. A financial memorandum must accompany each Bill on its introduction. In addition, there are statements from the Presiding Officer and the Executive on the Bill's legal competence - in other words, that the provisions are concerned only with devolved matters. Members' Bills do not have a competence statement from the Executive but may be accompanied by a financial memorandum.

b)   **Policy Memoranda** (e.g. SP Bill 4-PM) are produced only to accompany Executive Bills. They describe the objectives of the Bill, discuss alternative approaches and provide background to the consultation process.

Each stage of the Bill has an addendum to the title describing which version it is – [As Introduced], [As Amended at Stage …], [As Passed]. As the legislation applies to Scotland alone, the Bill title will include the territorial designation (i.e. Scotland) in round brackets. Bills should be cited as, for example, **SP Bill 23 Housing (Scotland) [as introduced] Bill Session 1 (2000)**.

The Passage of a Bill

The process of a Bill's passage through Parliament depends on the type of Bill but usually it consists of three stages, during which a careful examination of the principles and detailed provisions is made.

▶   Stage 1 - consideration of general principles and a decision whether they are agreed to (by Committee and by Parliament).

▶   Stage 2 - consideration of the details of the Bill (by Committee).

▶   Stage 3 - final consideration and a decision whether the Bill should be passed or rejected (by Parliament).

After the introduction of a Bill to Parliament, it is referred to the relevant Subject Committee (the 'Lead Committee') which considers the general principles and may take evidence. Other Committees may be involved and their views are submitted to the Lead Committee for inclusion in its report.

Once the Lead Committee has submitted its report on the particular Bill, the full Parliament has the opportunity to consider the general principles. If Parliament does not agree to the Bill's general principles, the Bill falls. A Bill can also be withdrawn during Stage 1 by the Member who introduced it. The Bill can be referred back to the Lead Committee for a further report and additional evidence can be taken. If the Parliament agrees with the general principles of a Bill, it proceeds to Stage 2, a careful 'line-by-line' scrutiny of its wording. This is done either entirely or partly by the Lead Committee and/or a Committee of the whole Parliament or another nominated Committee. Amendments can be made at this stage to alter provisions and influence the translation of policy into new legislation. Members can lodge proposals to change the wording of the text of a Bill and these normally appear in Section G of the following day's **Business Bulletin**.

A Marshalled List which includes all amendments proposed by Members is printed on the day Stage 2 begins (e.g. SP Bill 4-ML1). It should be noted that more than one Marshalled List of amendments for Stage 2 can appear (e.g. SP Bill 4-ML2, SP Bill 4-ML3). Once each section of the Bill has been considered, the amended Bill is reprinted, on purple-tinted paper (e.g. SP Bill 4A [As Amended At Stage 2]).

The Bill then returns to the full Parliament for further consideration and amendment (Stage 3). At this point, only those amendments selected for consideration by the Presiding Officer are printed as a Marshalled List (e.g. SP Bill 4A-ML). Parliament then debates and decides whether or not the Bill should be passed, based on the voting of at least a quarter of all MSPs. Up to half of the sections of the Bill may be referred back for further Stage 2 consideration by the relevant Committee(s) at this time. On the Bill's return to the Parliament, further amendments may be made only to those sections initially referred back to the Committee.

The Parliament finally considers whether or not to approve the Bill. Once passed, it is reprinted with the additional heading [As Passed] (e.g. SP Bill 4B) and presented to the Sovereign for Royal Assent. The period between the passing of a Bill and receipt of Royal Assent can be substantial because of the requirements of the devolution legislation which allow the Secretary of State and certain Law Officers the opportunity to intervene on grounds such as competence. Once Royal Assent is given the Bill becomes an Act of the Scottish Parliament (e.g. 2000 asp 5 Abolition of Feudal Tenure etc. (Scotland) Act 2000). There may be slight non-substantial differences between the 'As Passed' version of a Bill and its subsequent Act - for example, the numbering of sections.

In certain cases (i.e. Emergency Bills), the passage of the Bill can be subject to accelerated procedures whereby there is no committee report at Stage 1 and Stage 2 is taken by a 'Committee of the whole Parliament'. Such was the case with the Mental Health (Public Safety and Appeals) (Scotland) Bill.

All the bibliographic details for each version of Scottish Parliament Bills and their various accompanying papers are recorded in The Stationery Office publications, *Daily List* and *Weekly List*. The *Daily List* is also available on **The Stationery Office web-site** (http://www.clicktso.com/).

Passage of Bill Series

This is a series of publications from The Stationery Office designed to give a convenient and authoritative record of the Parliamentary proceedings leading to the enactment of Acts of the Scottish Parliament. By gathering together all the relevant material, these volumes should allow users to follow the proceedings in a straightforward way. The series is particularly useful in reproducing the wording of each amendment. The first volume (SPPB 1) deals with the passage of the Mental Health (Public Safety and Appeals) (Scotland) Bill 1999, which became the first Act of the Scottish Parliament. The intention is to publish each new volume around two months after the publication of the Act itself. A typical volume includes:

▶ every print of the Bill

▶ all accompanying documents (including the Explanatory Notes)

▶ all Marshalled List of amendments from Stages 2 and 3

▶ every Groupings list (i.e. groupings of amendments according to subject matter) from Stages 2 and 3

▶ the lead Committee's Stage 1 Report

▶ the Official Report of the Stage 1 and Stage 3 debates in the Parliament

▶ the Official Report of the Stage 2 debates in committee and

▶ the Minutes (or relevant extracts) of relevant committee and Parliament meetings for all three Stages.

All documents are reproduced in their original layout and page numbering. Resultant Acts are not included as these are generally available and are not Parliamentary publications.

To help understand this process, the passage of the **Abolition of Feudal Tenure etc. (Scotland) Bill** is given as an example (Fig. 1 (*over*)).

Fig. 1 Passage of Abolition of Feudal Tenure etc. (Scotland) Bill

		Stage 1				Stage 2
Title	Bill No.	Lead Committee	Debates	Stage 1 Report	Parliament Debate	Debates
Abolition of Feudal Tenure etc. (Scotland) Bill	4 (4-EN) (4-PM) 6/10/00	Justice and Home Affairs	9/11/99 17/11/99 1/12/99* 7/12/99*	SPP 44 , Session 1, 1999	15/12/99	15/3/00 21/3/00 29/3/00

* Indicates where Committee discussions were held in private so no official record of discussions is available.

	Stage 3			Passed	Royal Assent
Marshalled Lists	Bill No. (As Amended at Stage 2)	Parliament Debate	Marshalled Lists	Bill No. (As Passed)	Act No.
SP Bill 4-ML1, Session 1, 2000	4A	3/5/2000	4A-ML	4B (3/5/00)	asp. 5 (9/6/00)
SP Bill 4-ML2, Session 1, 2000					
SP Bill 4-ML3, Session 1, 2000					

Private Bills

Private Bills, promoted by an individual or a group outwith Parliament, are also a part of the legislative process. Detailed **guidance on private bills** (http://www.scottish.parliament .uk/official_report/cttee/private-01/gpb-c.htm) is available on the **Parliamentary Procedure** (http://www.scottish.parliament.uk/parl_bus/proced.html) section of the Parliament web-site. Private Bills differ from Public Bills in that they seek measures in the private interests of the promoters and there is much scrutiny to ensure such Bills are within the Parliament's legislative competence. They include 'works' Bills authorising the construction or alteration of certain classes of works, as well as personal Bills.

As all Bills that are enacted become Acts of the Scottish Parliament (ASPs), there is no distinction of type and private ASPs are numbered in the same single series as public ASPs. Once again, every Bill must be accompanied by Explanatory Notes, showing what each provision of the Bill does, and a Promoter's Memorandum is also required to explain the policy objectives of, and consultation process for, the Bill. In addition, each Private Bill must have a Promoter's statement detailing the process in the preparation and notification of the Bill, an Estimate of Expense, a Funding Statement and an agreement assigning copyright to the Scottish Parliamentary Corporate Body. 'Works' Bills may also require to be accompanied by maps, plans, sections and a book of reference.

All Private Bills will be subject to a three Stage process – a Preliminary Stage, when a Private Bill Committee considers the general principles and any objections, and decides whether it should proceed; a Consideration Stage, which involves the Committee taking evidence (including cross-examination) on the details of the Bill and considering amendments; and a Final Stage, when Parliament considers further amendments and decides whether or not to pass the Bill. A separate Reconsideration Stage is also possible in certain circumstances.

A Private Bill Committee, established by resolution of the Parliament, will consider such a Bill until it has received Royal Assent, falls or is withdrawn. It is considered likely that most Private Bill Committees will be of a quasi-judicial nature, arbitrating between competing private interests. As with Public Bills, a Private Bill introduced in any session of the Parliament falls if it has not been passed by the Parliament before the end of that session. However, unlike Public Bills, Private Bills which fall can be 'carried over' to the following session.

Members' Bills
(http://www.scottish.parliament.uk/parl_bus/membill.htm)

Any Member can introduce up to two Member's Bills in any one session and, if supported by eleven other Members, these can be introduced before the full Parliament.

These are recorded in Section G of the **Business Bulletin**. Information on **Proposed Members' Bills** is also available on the Parliament web-site (http://www.scottish. parliament.uk/parl_bus/membill.htm). This page lists all Bills proposed by Members since the beginning of the current Parliamentary session in their order of lodging. It indicates the wording of the proposed Bill, the date on which the proposal acquired its eleventh supporter, the total number of supporters and whether or not the Bill has been introduced to Parliament.

The **Documents** (http://www.scottish.parliament.uk/parl_bus/pab.html) section of the Parliament web-site contains information on **Bills** (http://www.scottish. parliament.uk/parl_bus/legis.html). This page lists Bills In Progress, those currently going through the Parliament and links to those **Not in Progress** (http://www.scottish.parliament.uk/parl_bus/bill-final.htm), those which have passed or fallen. This page also provides a link to **Proposed Members Bills** (http://www.scottish.parliament.uk/parl_bus/membill.htm) which lists all Bills proposed by Members in the current Parliamentary session.

Section K of the current **Business Bulletin** (http://www.scottish.parliament.uk/ agenda_and_decisions/forth.html#currentbb) contains information on the progress of Parliamentary business. The current edition of **What's Happening in the Scottish Parliament (WHISP)** (http://www.scottish.parliament.uk/whats_ happening/whisp.html) contains a cumulative list of Bills and Laid Papers.

For more information on the passage of Bills through the Scottish Parliament, see **Fact File No.3 How The Scottish Parliament Works (Section on Bills)** (http://www.scottish.parliament.uk/welcoming_you/ff3.htm#bill).

Acts of the Scottish Parliament
(http://www.scotland-legislation.hmso.gov.uk/legislation/scotland/s-acts.htm)

Acts are laws passed by the Parliament which have received Royal Assent from the Sovereign - in other words, the stage in the legislative process when the approval of the Sovereign turns a Bill into an Act. Acts are printed under the authority of the Queen's Printer for Scotland and are published shortly after being given Royal Assent. Acts of the Scottish Parliament are published in a numbered sequence within a calendar year (e.g. 2000 asp 5 Abolition of Feudal Tenure etc. (Scotland) Act 2000). The aim is to publish them electronically simultaneously or at least within 24 hours of their publication in printed form. Some more complex Acts may take longer to appear. A record of their publication appears in The Stationery Office publications, *Daily List* and *Weekly List*. The Stationery Office publishes bound, indexed compilations of the Acts of the Scottish Parliament. The first volume covered the thirteen acts from 1999 to 2000.

Explanatory notes
(http://www.scotland-legislation.hmso.gov.uk/legislation/scotland/s-exp-pa.htm)

Explanatory Notes, prepared by the Department responsible for the subject matter of the Act, often accompany Acts resulting from Bills introduced by Scottish Ministers. These are published separately from the Act itself and their purpose is to make the Act accessible to readers who are not legally qualified and who have no specialised knowledge of the matters dealt with. They are intended to allow the reader to grasp what the Act sets out to achieve and place its effect in context. They explain the wording of the relevant act section by section. The aim is to publish the Notes electronically at the same time as the Act but, again, there may be a delay of some days.

Acts of the Scottish Parliament are accessible from the HMSO web-site (http://www.scotland-legislation.hmso.gov.uk/legislation/scotland/s-acts.htm) and not the Parliament web-site. They are listed by year and then by Act number.

Explanatory Notes (http://www.scotland-legislation.hmso.gov.uk/legislation/ scotland/s-exp-pa.htm) are also available on the HMSO web-site. The notes are arranged in alphabetical order on the web-site.

The HMSO web-site also contains other useful information for users of Scottish statutory materials. The **United Kingdom Legislation** (http://www.legislation.hmso. gov.uk/) site includes the full text of all legislation enacted by the UK Parliament whether this applies to the United Kingdom as a whole or only to constituent parts of the UK (e.g. Scotland). The **Links to the Scotland Act 1998 and Associated Delegated Legislation** (http://www.scotland-legislation.hmso.gov.uk/legislation/ scotland/scotact.htm) site provides links to the Scotland Act and the associated Statutory Instruments which established the Scottish Parliament and the Scottish Executive.

There is a search engine on the Acts of the Scottish Parliament web-site but it should be used with caution! The search engine will retrieve items from the whole **HMSO Legislation** (http://www.hmso.gov.uk/legis.htm) database. This means that all statutory materials (acts, explanatory notes and statutory instruments) from the Westminster Parliament, the Welsh and Northern Ireland Assemblies, as well as the Scottish Parliament, will be searched simultaneously.

Scottish Statutory Instruments (SSIs)
(http://www.scotland-legislation.hmso.gov.uk/legislation/scotland/s-stat.htm)

Much of the technical detail of legislation is not included within the sections of an Act. Acts can confer powers on the Scottish Ministers to introduce a wide range of secondary, delegated or subordinate legislation in the form of administrative regulations, amendments, revocations and orders which appear as Scottish Statutory Instruments. They are equally a part of the law as the original Act. These can be laid before Parliament for its approval but in many instances this is not necessary. Certain Statutory Instruments are not formally published because of their limited local effect. These local Instruments frequently relate to traffic or similar regulations and are recorded in the Stationery Office's *Daily List* and *Weekly List*, as well as the annual Stationery Office list *Scottish Parliamentary and Statutory Publications*. Affirmative instruments require Parliamentary approval, negative instruments will come into force unless Parliament reject them. There is a group of Statutory Instruments called Commencement Orders which bring into force the whole or part of an Act of Parliament. These are now separately identified in the *Daily List* and *Weekly List*. Scottish Statutory Instruments can implement European Union directives and can be revoked by subsequent SSIs. They are published with explanatory notes and include references to the relevant legislation which gives the enabling powers, as well as the dates when the SSIs are made, laid before Parliament and come into force. They appear individually and are numbered consecutively within a calendar year (e.g. **The Human Rights Act 1998 (Jurisdiction) (Scotland) Rules 2000 No. 301**). Annual compilations will appear eventually as bound and indexed volumes. Readers should remember that any Statutory Instrument of a more general application might have an effect on the law in Scotland.

Scottish Statutory Instruments (SSIs) are accessible from the HMSO web-site (http://www.scotland-legislation.hmso.gov.uk/legislation/scotland/s-acts.htm) and **not** the Parliament web-site, They are listed by year and then by SSI number. SSIs are published in full text form on the web-site as they become available. Note that draft SSIs (i.e. instruments laid before Parliament for approval by resolution) are not available on this site at present.

Also worth noting on the Scottish Legislation web-site is the **Links to the Scotland Act 1998 and Associated Delegated Legislation** (http://www.scotland-legislation. hmso.gov.uk/legislation/scotland/scotact.htm) site. This provides links to the Scotland Act and the associated Statutory Instruments which established the Scottish Parliament and the Scottish Executive.

There is a search engine on the Scottish Statutory Instruments web-site. However, it should be used with caution! The search engine will retrieve items from the whole **HMSO Legislation** (http://www.hmso.gov.uk/legis.htm) database. This means that all statutory materials (acts, explanatory notes and statutory instruments) from the Westminster Parliament, the Welsh and Northern Ireland Assemblies, as well as the Scottish Parliament, will be searched simultaneously.

Publications from the Scottish Parliament

Apart from Bills, Acts and Scottish Statutory Instruments, with their explanatory notes and memoranda, there is a wide range of other publications emanating from the Parliament. These can be viewed on the **Documents** (http://www.scottish.parliament.uk/ parl_bus/pab.html) section of the Parliament Web-site and are available in hard copy from The Stationery Office.

These Parliamentary publications are:

Business Bulletin
(http://www.scottish.parliament.uk/agenda_and_decisions/forth.html#currentbb)

This comprehensive guide to current parliamentary business is considered to be the key working document and the authoritative publication on parliamentary business. It is produced on a daily basis, Monday to Friday, while Parliament is sitting. It has a running number for each calendar year and comprises various sections (see below) which detail different aspects of the Parliament's business. The printed version appears unrevised and ends with a list of telephone contact numbers and web-site addresses, which gives access to Committee proceedings. It does not have an index.

Presently, the individual sections of the **Business Bulletin** are:

▶ Announcements - usually made by the Presiding Officer on the days when Parliament sits (normally Wednesdays and Thursdays) and include notification of Royal Assent, dates of by-elections and certain procedural information for Members.

▶ Section A: Daily Business List - appears on the days when either the full Parliament or any one of its Committees meet. On these days, a detailed timetable of the day's business is published. The list includes such information as the location and times of Committee meetings and a list of witnesses appearing before Committees on that day. On Thursdays, the programme of Parliamentary business for the following two weeks is recorded.

▶ Section B: Business Programme - the agreed programme of business for the following two weeks, including timings.

▶ Section C: Agendas of Committee Meetings - including dates and locations of meetings.

▶ Section D: Oral Questions - Oral questions are listed on Tuesdays and Thursdays. On Tuesdays, a list of questions selected for answer by the First Minister on the following Thursday are listed (S1F); those listed on Thursdays, (S1O) are selected for answer the following Thursday. On those later dates, the questions appear in the same order in the Daily Business List. All questions are prefaced by the name of the Member asking. Up to three questions are selected for answer at Open Question Time and up to thirty questions for Question Time, the latter are selected randomly. Any other questions not selected do not appear in the Bulletin and are not answered. Ministers cannot be questioned about reserved matters.

▶ Section E: Written Questions - these are lodged by Members on the preceding business day and are arranged by running number (e.g. S1W -12552). Questions allow Members to obtain information, figures and statistics from the Executive on all aspects of policy and action. Answers to written questions are normally given within fourteen days and are published in the **Written Answers of the Official Report**.

▶ Section F: Motions and Amendments - a record of all motions presented by Members including business motions put forward on behalf of the Parliamentary Bureau. They appear in reverse running number order (e.g. S1M-1419). The wording, date of lodging, supporters and any amendments are recorded. Motions are removed from the **Bulletin** when they are to be taken by Parliament, when the Bureau decides that they should not be debated or if they have appeared for one month and have not been chosen for inclusion in a future business motion. The full text of all outstanding motions and amendments appear in the **Bulletin** every Monday.

▶ Section G: Bills - including amendments to Bills and proposals for Member's Bills. Bills attracting eleven supporters can be introduced before Parliament.

▶ Section H: New Documents - a wide range of documents are laid before the Parliament, including Executive Papers, Committee Reports and Statutory Instruments.

▶ Section I: Petitions - made to the Parliament by an individual or a body of people. They are given a running number (e.g. PE 36).

▶ Section J: Parliamentary Bureau: – a note of decisions taken at meetings.

▶ Section K: Progress of Parliamentary Business - this provides a record of the progress of all Bills before Parliament and of subordinate legislation (Scottish Statutory Instruments). For subordinate legislation, the number of Instrument, Lead Committee and the date of its laying are given. Dates of the next meeting of each Committee are also recorded. Further information for this section can be found on the relevant web-site.

The web version of the **Business Bulletin** (http://www.scottish.parliament.uk/ agenda_and_decisions/forth.html) follows the format of the printed copy.

The home page of the **Business Bulletin** provides links to the current Bulletin and all previous Bulletins for that calendar year by month. At the bottom of the page there are links to the archived Bulletins of previous years.

> The **Business Bulletin** has no index. However, it is possible to search it using the Scottish Parliament web-site **search engine** (http://www.scottish.parliament.uk/ search.html). Make sure that you click on the box marked 'Business Bulletins'. This will limit searches to only that database. For more detailed advice on how to use the Scottish Parliament web-site search engine effectively, go to **Guide to Searching** (http://www.scottish.parliament.uk/help.htm).

Minutes of Proceedings
(http://www.scottish.parliament.uk/official_report/meeting.html)

This is the legal, official record of the day's business and the decisions taken by the Parliament produced on a daily basis. They record voting figures on motions and amendments. Frequently, an appendix of subordinate legislation laid before Parliament and Committee Reports is attached to the Minutes. The Minutes appear irregularly and are arranged chronologically within volume numbers but these bear no relation to other series (e.g. volume 1 runs to 11 May 2000, while volume 2 commences 17 May 2000).

> **Minutes of Proceedings** (http://www.scottish.parliament.uk/official_report/ meeting.html) can be found on the Meetings of Parliament section of the web-site. They are listed in reverse chronological order, within volume number. The format is similar to the printed version, however it appears as one continuous page so be careful if you are printing from this version!

Official Report: Plenary Sessions of the Parliament
(http://www.scottish.parliament.uk/official_report/meeting.html)

The remit of the **Official Report** is to produce a substantially verbatim report, in both electronic and printed form, of the proceedings of every meeting of Parliament by 8.00 AM on the following day, detailing the debates and decisions of the day. Initially, it was envisaged that a bound volume of the daily editions would be published approximately every month as the definitive edition, containing written answers to parliamentary questions and an index. However, in November 2000, the Parliamentary Corporate Body decided that the archive edition will be published electronically in CD-Rom format only and no bound volumes will be produced. At present, it is thought that the cumulative CD-Rom version is likely to be produced three times a year and it is likely that the CD-Rom for 1999-2000 will be published in a single volume. It is very important to remember that the **Official Report** has no printed index but it is expected that the CD version will have a fully searchable index. Note that the CD version will contain not only the Official Report of the Plenary Sessions of the Parliament and of Committees but also the Written Answers Report. The inclusion of other Parliamentary publications and enhanced searching facilities are likely to be future developments.

The individual printed issues of the Report are headed 'Meeting of the Parliament' and have the date of the sitting covered. Each issue is prefaced with a record of the day's business and a list of the MSPs speaking to the motions before the Parliament. Oral answers to Oral Questions are also recorded here, arranged alphabetically by topic. Text of the debates is arranged in two columns on the page and the numbering of pages runs through the whole series of issues of a volume of the Report.

To begin with, the timing of the volume number change was determined by the number of meetings of the Parliament but from April 2001, all volumes of the **Official Report** are no longer numbered and carry the date only. Usually, a volume covers a period of between four and six weeks, coinciding approximately with a sitting period of the Parliament. Each volume begins with a record of the ministers, conveners and other key figures. The name of the MSP and the time of speaking head contributions to debates. All votes on motions and amendments are listed, along with a record of how each MSP voted. Corrections to issues of the **Official Report** appear at the end of later issues. The correct citation for an entry in the **Official Report** is, for example, SP OR 17 May 2001, col 769.

> The **Official Report** (http://www.scottish.parliament.uk/official_report/meeting.html) on the web provides links to all Official Reports of the Parliament from 1999 onwards.
>
> The **Official Reports** are listed in reverse chronological order, starting with the most recent report. Only the current year's reports are listed, with a link at the bottom to previous years (which includes the 'definitive editions' see below). Like the printed version, each issue is prefaced with a record of the day's business and a list of the MSPs speaking to the motions before the Parliament. Oral answers to Oral Questions are also recorded here, arranged alphabetically by topic. However, the text of the debates in the web version appears as a single, continuous page. Be careful if you are printing from this version! Column numbers, representing their equivalent in the printed version, appear on the left-hand side of the page.
>
> The definitive editions of the **Official Report** are known as *Scottish Parliament Volumes*. The 'definitive' edition is the final 'corrected' version of the **Official Report**, including Written Answers. They are issued in volumes, each one covering approximately six weeks. These are published in electronic format only.
>
> The **Official Report** has no index. However, it is possible to search for information on a particular topic by using the Scottish Parliament web-site **search engine** (http://www.scottish.parliament.uk/search.html). Make sure that you click on the box marked 'Official Report'. This will limit your search to only that database. For more detailed advice on how to use the Scottish Parliament web-site search engine effectively, go to **Guide to Searching** (http://www.scottish.parliament.uk/help.htm).

Written Answers Report
(http://www.scottish.parliament.uk/official_report/pq.html)

In addition to the substantially verbatim report of proceedings, Written Answers to Parliamentary Questions come under the remit of the Official Report. These are considered one of the most important and heavily used parliamentary documents. Written Questions are normally answered within fourteen days and these are published as a weekly compilation but a significant difference with the electronic version is that Answers are posted on the Parliament web-site as they are supplied. The printed copy is prefaced by a contents list arranged alphabetically by subject. Issues also include questions which were selected for oral answer but which were not reached, along with their answers Frequently, Written Answers provide much detail on all aspects of policy and are a valuable source of information on costs and statistics which may not always be available elsewhere (e.g. the number of available staffed beds in each Health Board area for five categories of patient for each year 1995-1999 - S1W-405; answer in Written Answers, vol.1, no.7, pp.92-94).

To begin with, the timing of the change in volume number was determined by the number of written answers and did **not** follow the numbering of the Official Report. However, from April 2001, all volumes of the Official Report are no longer numbered and carry the date only. Each volume does cover, however, a similar period of usually four to six weeks. The correct citation for a reference to Written Answers is, for example, SP WA 10 May 2001, p 151.

The Written Answers Report (http://www.scottish.parliament.uk/official_report/pq.html) on the web provides links to all reports from 1999 onwards. At the top of the page are links to the Daily Written Answers, these appear only on the web, and are produced in advance of the Written Answers Report which are published weekly. The format for both is similar - a listing of questions, arranged alphabetically, by topic, in one continuous page. Be careful if you are printing from this version!

At the foot of the web-page there are links to the 'definitive' edition of the Official Report, known as *Scottish Parliament Volumes*. The 'definitive' edition is the final 'corrected' version of the Official Report, includes the Written Answers. They are issued in volumes, each one covering approximately six weeks.

The Written Answers Report has no index. However, it is possible to locate written answers by using the Written Parliamentary Questions and Answers database search engine (http://www.scottish.parliament.uk/webapp/search_PQ). Using the template provided, enter search terms in one or more of the fields or select from the drop-down lists. There is an instructional guide to searching parliamentary questions and answers at http://www.scottish.parliament.uk/help-pq.htm.

Official Report: Committee Sessions
(http://www.scottish.parliament.uk/official_report/cttee.html)

The work of the individual Committees is an extremely important part of the Scottish Parliament and a wide range of issues come before them. Committee work includes consideration of Scottish Statutory Instruments and other subordinate legislation, Petitions, European documents and the first two stages of Bills. Each one of the eighteen Committees produces an Official Report and Minutes of Proceedings for each meeting held. An agenda and any papers required for meetings are produced in advance of the meeting and are made available on the web-site of the individual Committees. Please note that these documents are only available on the web and are issued in pdf format.

To help understand the work of a Committee, an example of the passage of the Report into the EU Charter of Fundamental Rights through the European Committee is provided in Fig. 2 *(over)*.

Fig. 2: Report into the EU Charter of Fundamental Rights - 2nd Report 20 **Committee system**

25/1/00	22/2/00	28/11/00
European Committee Official Report No.2 Session 1999-2000	**European Committee** Official Report No. 4 Session 2000	**European Committee***
The Committee discussed and agreed the details of its Forward Work Programme for January 2000 to June 2001 as laid out in paper **EU/00/2/1.** This work programme identified twelve issues that the Committee agreed to progress, using a system of nominated `reporters' who would conduct the study and develop the report on the Committee's behalf. Dennis Canavan appointed reporter for The European Union Charter of Fundamental Rights.	Dennis Canavan brought forward his 'terms of reference' for The Proposed European Charter on Fundamental Rights: development of a Scottish perspective **(EU/00/4/2)** which were approved without amendment.	The Committee discussed **(in private)** the draft Reporter's Report **(EU/00/20/4)** on this subject. It was agreed that the Convener and the Reporter (Dennis Canavan) would meet subsequent to the Committee meeting to refine the conclusions. A revised draft would be brought to the next available Committee meeting.

*Indicates where Committee discussions were held in private so no official record of discussions is available.

Note also that all papers with EU prefixes (e.g. **(EU/00/4/2)**) were private Committee documents and are not available in hard copy or via the Committee's web-site.

12/12/00	16/1/01	07/02/01
European Committee*	European Committee*	European Committee

The Committee discussed (**in private**) the draft Reporter's Report (**EU/00/21/7**) by Dennis Canavan on this subject. The Committee agreed a number of revisions and agreed to discuss a revised report at a subsequent meeting.	The Committee discussed (**in private**) and agreed in principle the draft Reporter's Report (**EU/01/01/06**) by Dennis Canavan on this subject and agreed to mandate the Convenor, the Reporter and the Clerk to make any minor, inconsequential amendments or typographical errors before printing and issuing the document as a formal Committee Report and inviting the response of the Scottish Executive.	**Report into the EU Charter of Human Rights** (**SPP 260, Session 1 2001**)

The layout of the Official Report of meetings of the individual Committees follows that of full Parliamentary meetings but the individual printed issues have no numbering system, other than the number of the meeting within that calendar year. The printed version of the report of each meeting is available before the next meeting of that Committee. Each issue lists the membership and other people attending (including witnesses and non-Committee MSPs who may have a local interest) on the day as well as the agenda. When discussion is held in private, the deliberations are not reported. The Report records votes, and how members voted, on proposed amendments to Bills. The correct citation for a reference to a Committee Report is, for example, SP OR RD 8 May 2001, col 1997.

It is important to note that all three printed elements of the Official Report stand unrevised and the only corrected version is the electronic archive in CD-Rom format.

The Official Report: Committee Sessions (http://www.scottish.parliament.uk/official_report/cttee.html) section of the Parliament web-site has links to the home pages of each Committee. Each home page lists the convenor, membership and remit of the Committee, as well as direct links to all reports and papers produced by them. About half way down the page you will find information about, and links to, the Committees Official Report and Minutes of Proceedings, as well as any agenda and papers (which appear only on the web). They are listed by date, in reverse chronological order.

Like the printed version, each issue is prefaced with a record of the day's business and a list of the MSPs speaking to the motions before the Parliament. However, the text of the debates in the web version appears as a single, continuous page. Be careful if you are printing from this version! Column numbers, representing their equivalent in the printed version, appear on the left-hand side of the page.

The Official Report: Committee Sessions has no index. However, it is possible to search for information on a particular topic by using the Scottish Parliament web-site search engine (http://www.scottish.parliament.uk/search.htm). Make sure that you click on the box marked 'All Committees'. This will limit searches to only that database. Please note however, this will search the whole of the Committee section of the database and will return hits on Committee Reports, Minutes, etc. For more detailed advice on how to use the Scottish Parliament web-site search engine effectively, go to Guide to Searching (http://www.scottish.parliament.uk/help.htm).

A very important point to remember is that there is no dedicated section of the Scottish Parliament web-site solely devoted to Parliament Papers. A general search of the web-site for a specific paper cannot be restricted to Scottish Parliament Papers only. Searching, therefore, can be a frustrating and lengthy process. Since most Parliament Papers emanate from Committees, restricting the search by clicking on the Committee box will limit the number of hits significantly.

At present, the vast majority of Scottish Parliament (SP) Papers have been the reports of individual Committee enquiries into subjects coming under their remits (e.g. Bills, subordinate legislation, petitions). SP Papers are given a running number as they are published within a particular four-year session of Parliament, with the year of publication in brackets (e.g. SPP 55, Session 1 (1999)). Papers also have a numbering sequence relating to the relevant Committee, consisting of a Committee code, the year and a sequential Committee report number (e.g. EO/99/R1 – 1st report, 1999 of the Equal Opportunities Committee). They appear in no set order and so the reports of individual Committees will be spread through the sequence. The one assured way to find the papers issued by a particular Committee in printed form is to use the index to the annual list issued by the Stationery Office. When citing a Committee Report issued as a Scottish Parliament Paper, the correct form is, for example, Justice 1 Committee 2nd report, 2001, Stage 1 Report on the Convention Rights (Compliance) (Scotland) Bill (SPP 290) p 2036.

Reports will give the conclusions and recommendations based on Committee deliberations. They can include extracts from minutes of Committee proceedings, as well as oral and written evidence. They also reprint the Official Report of the relevant meeting of the Committee (e.g. Report on Stracathro Petition PE13. SPP 48. Session 1 (1999) includes the complete Official Report of the Health and Community Care Committee of 24 November 1999 when evidence was taken). Reports on subordinate legislation, particularly when no recommendations are made, tend to be brief notices.

Major enquiries that consider large amounts of evidence may appear in several volumes. Where a report splits into more than one volume, each volume retains the same SP Paper number (e.g. Education, Culture and Sport Committee. 11th Report 2000. Exam Results Inquiry. Vol.1 Minutes, Vol.2 Evidence. SPP 234. Session 1 (2000)).

Exceptions to the Committee reports in this sequence are the annual reports of the Corporate Body, including Parliament statistics, the Parliamentary and Health Service Ombudsman, consultation papers from the Standards Committee and certain requested reports laid before Parliament by Scottish Ministers (e.g. Report of the Inquiry into the Care and Treatment of Noel Ruddle. SPP 98. Session 1 (2000)). One particularly important annual report is that of the Parliamentary Committees, which reviews each committee's work over the year. These reports do appear in the **Documents** (http://www.scottish.parliament.uk/parl_bus/pab.html) section of the Parliament web-site.

WHISP (What's Happening in the Scottish Parliament)
(http://www.scottish.parliament.uk/whats_happening/whisp.html)

A weekly digest of information on the activities and work of the Parliament compiled by SPICe and designed for the general user. This publication records what has and will happen in the Parliament, usually covering a three week period. It lists the forthcoming business for the Parliament and its Committees and provides a summary of the previous week's business of the individual committees and the plenary meetings of the Parliament (including the results of all voting at division). In addition, WHISP contains a list of all Executive and Members Bills (arranged alphabetically), with a record of the Lead Committee and a timetable of the stages reached for each; a record of all papers laid before Parliament for that period; a progress report on all petitions being discussed and a record of Committee membership. WHISP is not a formal document and carries a varied range of material, such as a very useful list of Scottish Parliament Information Centre (SPICe) research notes and papers, a bibliography of Scottish Parliament publications which is cumulative by term, a record of a state of the political parties in the Parliament (including a detailed breakdown of voting at by-elections) and addresses and web-sites of parties and parliamentary staff. Frequently, WHISP provides a valuable abstract for new research notes and papers. When changes are made at the Scotland Office or there are significant developments in the relationship between the Scottish Executive and UK government departments, these appear in WHISP under Devolution Developments.

Cumulative lists of Bills, Laid Papers and Petitions, as well as a basic index to significant items in WHISP have appeared in issues prior to any recess of Parliament. The index is **not** cumulative. The first sixteen issues of WHISP contained a useful alphabetical glossary of terms used in Parliament and the various official publications. Other features in WHISP include the Labour/Liberal Democrat 'coalition' agreement (Partnership for Scotland), notices of ministerial changes in the Scottish government, important visitors to the Parliament, selections of statistics on the work of the Parliament (e.g. number of Written Questions answered) and a series of reviews of the Scottish regions. There are articles written by staff of the Information Centre on Partner Libraries and Documentation Centres. WHISP is the one exception to the general rule about citation of publications which applies equally to both electronic and printed versions of documents. In the case of WHISP at present, page numbers are not visible on the web.

Whats Happening in the Scottish Parliament (WHISP) (http://www.scottish. parliament.uk/whats_happening/whisp.html) follows the format of the printed copy. A contents page links to individual sections (Cumulative list of Bills, Petitions, SPICe Research Publications etc.). The home page of **WHISP** provides links to the current WHISP and all previous WHISP for that calendar year. At the bottom of the page there are links to the archived WHISPs of previous years.

It is not possible to restrict a search of the **Parliament web-site** (http://www.scottish. parliament.uk/search.html) to WHISP only, so searching for a topic in WHISP can be a frustrating and lengthy procedure. For more detailed advice on how to use the Scottish Parliament web-site search engine effectively, go to **Guide to Searching** (http://www.scottish.parliament.uk/help.htm).

Other publications

Committee Newsletters

At present, only one Committee publishes a newsletter, *Europe Matters* providing a range of information on the work of the European Committee. It is only available electronically in pdf format and requires an Acrobat Reader.

Cross-Party Groups
(http://www.scottish.parliament.uk/msps/cpg.html)

Cross-Party groups contain members from across the political parties who share an interest in a particular subject or cause. They can also include people from outside the Parliament. The Standards Committee formally regulates the groups since they can have an influential role within Parliament. The **Register of Cross-Party Groups** (http://www.scottish.parliament.uk/msps/cpg/cpg-reg.html) lists all groups, whether approved or awaiting approval. There are groups on such matters as the Scottish contemporary music industry, deafness, rail services for Scotland, and refugees and asylum seekers. Under each group is a record of member MSPs and others, as well as the group's purpose and links to the minutes of group meetings.

Parliamentary and Committee News Releases

News releases are a valuable source of information across the range of Parliamentary (http://www.scottish.parliament.uk/whats_happening/new.html) and Committee (http://www.scottish.parliament.uk/whats_happening/new.html#comm) activities. These are available only on the Parliament web-site and are listed in reverse chronological order. Archive lists of previous years' releases are appended to the current list. News releases about the activities of MSPs who are Ministers, or other government news, can be found on the **Scottish Executive web-site news pages** (http://www.scotland.gov.uk/news2/current.asp).

| Background Publications relevant to the Scottish Parliament |

Factfiles (http://www.scottish.parliament.uk/whats_happening/research/factfiles.html) are a series of background leaflets produced by the Scottish Parliament Public Information Office which give information on such matters as the devolved Parliament, the Scottish parliamentary tradition, the working of the Parliament, the relationship between constituents and MSPs, and guidance on the submission of public petitions.

In the first year of operation, the Parliament Chamber Office and the Clerking Services Directorate published a series of **guides** (http://www.scottish.parliament.uk/parl_bus/proced.html) to various processes (e.g. **Detailed Guidance on Motions**). These are intended to support and expand on Standing Orders and are aimed principally at helping MSPs and the staff of the Parliament All these publications are available in printed and electronic formats.

SPICe Research Publications
(http://www.scottish.parliament.uk/whats_happening/research/subj_indx.htm)

The Scottish Parliament Information Centre (SPICe) produces a wide range of research notes and papers providing short overviews (notes) or more in-depth analyses (papers) of matters of interest to MSPs. All of these are impartial, unlike policy memoranda or consultation papers which reflect the political intent of the party of government. Notes cover such topics as poverty, fox hunting, organ donation and transplantation, while there have been research papers on land reform, housing stock transfers and freedom of information. SPICe has also produced series of publications on the parliament, devolved areas and devolution. All research publications can be viewed on the Parliament's web-site at http://www.scottish.parliament.uk/whats_happening/research/subj_indx.htm and are available on request from Partner Libraries.

Annual List of Scottish Parliamentary and Statutory Publications

Every year, the Stationery Office publishes an annual list of *Scottish Parliamentary and Statutory Publications*. It is one of the few relevant printed publications with an index but it usually appears six months after the end of the year of coverage. Publications are listed by type (e.g. Bills) and are arranged usually by sequential number.

Holyrood: the magazine for Scotland's Parliament

Although this is commercially produced, this fortnightly magazine provides a user-friendly and valuable guide to parliamentary business. Each issue contains a digest insert (known as the Blue Pages) recording parliamentary business, cross-party group meetings, questions and committee meetings. It also carries profiles of MSPs, interviews with key figures in national bodies and a range of articles relevant to policy and the major issues of government. For readers who are familiar with the Westminster parliament, it is similar in style and content to *The House Magazine*.

Official Publications from the Scottish Executive

T he legislation that established a Scottish Parliament also made provision for the creation of an administrative arm of government for devolved matters – the Scottish Executive and the Scottish Administration, although the corporate identity is described as the **Scottish Executive** (http://www.scotland.gov.uk). It assumed the functions of the former Scottish Office and its associated departments and is under the direction and control of the First Minister, his Scottish Ministers and the Scottish Law Officers (i.e. the Lord Advocate and the Solicitor General for Scotland). In effect, this is the Civil Service for the Scottish Parliament and, together with Finance and Central Services and Corporate Services, consists of six major departments:

▶ **Development** (http://www.scotland.gov.uk/who/dept_development.asp) (covering such matters as housing, planning and regeneration, local government, transport and social inclusion issues),

▶ **Education** (http://www.scotland.gov.uk/who/dept_education.asp) (including such matters as sports policy, arts and cultural heritage),

▶ **Enterprise and Lifelong Learning** (http://www.scotland.gov.uk/who/elld) (including economics, training and industrial affairs),

▶ **Environment and Rural Affairs** (http://www.scotland.gov.uk/who/ dept_rural.asp) (including agriculture, environmental matters and fisheries),

▶ **Health** (http://www.scotland.gov.uk/who/dept_health.asp),

▶ **Justice** (http://www.scotland.gov.uk/who/dept_justice.asp) (including the Scottish Courts Service, prisons, fire services).

Within each department, there can be sub-divisions into Groups, Directorates and Units (e.g. Rural Partnership for Change National Steering Group) to deal with the specific responsibilities of the overall departmental remit. Each of these sub-divisions can produce documents which may be regarded as Official Publications and a reader can be presented with a bewildering array of reports, consultation papers, news releases, guidelines and bulletins. Publications from the Scottish Executive can be produced jointly with other bodies both within and outwith Scotland (e.g. *Capercaillie: a review of research needs* was published by the Executive, the Forestry Commission and Scottish Natural Heritage). In addition, an individual Division, Group or Unit can author publications. Regardless of the particular sub-division responsible, most documents of substance now have an ISBN with a Scottish Executive 0 75592 prefix.

In addition to the major Departments, there are ten Agencies responsible to the Scottish Executive for certain specific matters ranging from fisheries research to HM Inspectorate of Education. Publications from these Agencies frequently are not authored by the Executive and, therefore, do not appear on the Executive web-site. Agency publications are discussed with those of other public bodies in Chapter 6.

At present, the policy of the Executive is for all publications to be available on the Scottish Executive web-site (http://www.scotland.gov.uk/publications/recent.asp). However, users should be aware that there are a few exceptions to this. These include some important papers, for example the White Paper on Civil Marriages Outwith Registration Offices, which is only available from the General Register Office, Scotland web-site. All Scottish Executive publications are available from the contracted sales and distribution agent, The Stationery Office Bookshop in Edinburgh.

There are two exceptions to this – circulars, and consultation papers and their responses. Circulars can be obtained from the relevant Department, while consultation papers can be viewed in the Scottish Executive Library and Information Services Centre at Saughton House in Edinburgh.

The Scottish Executive Library and Information Services (SELIS) produce an annual list of publications authored by the Scottish Executive and received in the Library. It includes bibliographic details and is available both in paper format and on the Executive web-site. It is probably the most comprehensive source for this material and gives web addresses for many of the items listed. The publications are arranged by responsible unit or Department and by type (e.g. consultation papers, circulars). Within each grouping, the publications are listed in alphabetical order. As it the key source for Scottish Executive publishing, its arrangement has been used for the discussion of the paper versions of documents, although not in the same order. The paper version has a title index.

Users can also find details of Executive publications in recognised national listings such as UKOP and Justis Parlianet or the printed *Catalogue of British Official Publications Not Published by The Stationery Office* produced by Chadwyck-Healey.

Scottish Executive Papers (SE Papers)

Many, if not most, documents laid before the Scottish Parliament are presented as a courtesy rather than through a formal legal obligation. The Scottish Ministers lay these as Scottish Executive (SE) Papers. Some of these papers can also be House of Commons Papers (e.g. Criminal Injuries Compensation Authority Annual Report and Accounts 1999/2000 is HC 356 and SE/2001/87). The variety of material within the SE Paper sequence is wide and can be confusing. In general, SE Papers include:

- ▶ Annual reports of Executive Agencies, Commissioners appointed under the terms of certain Acts, Scottish public bodies, including further education colleges, NHS Trusts in Scotland and water authorities, and cross-border public authorities who are responsible to the Scottish Executive for their activities in Scotland (e.g. British Waterways),

- ▶ Key statistical publications, including the Annual Report of the Registrar General for Scotland, Scottish Economic Reports, Scottish Economic Statistics and Scottish Social Statistics (see Chapter 7),

- ▶ Scottish Law Commission documents (which also appear as Command Papers),

- ▶ Guarantees made by the Scottish Ministers under the National Health Service (Scotland) Act on NHS Trusts borrowing sums of money,

- ▶ Reports by Scottish Ministers under the orders of sections of certain Acts (e.g. Local Government Finance (Scotland) Order 2001, SE/2001/64 regarding the Revenue Support Grant; special grant reports on monies paid to local authorities),

- ▶ National Audit Office reports (e.g. *Scottish Enterprise: skillseekers training for young people*, SE/2000/19),

- ▶ Joint responses to transport and environmental programmes, frequently co-ordinated by the Department of the Environment, Transport and the Regions,

- ▶ Other major policy position papers (e.g. *The Way Forward for Care*, SE/2000/67), reviews and consultation documents (e.g. *An Open Scotland: freedom of information*, SE/1999/51).

Other valuable statistical material can be found in the SE Paper sequence. In addition to the annual *Scottish Local Government Financial Statistics,* Scottish Natural Heritage, a Non-Departmental Public Body, produces a volume of Facts and Figures to accompany the annual report.

It is important to note that The Stationery Office publishes very few SE Papers. Besides the annual reports of public bodies, the vast bulk of the Scottish Executive material is published by the Executive itself. Some of the early reports from NHS Trusts can look more like newspapers than official papers. Many Papers do not carry an SE Paper serial number or any indication that they are, in fact, part of the SE Paper sequence (e.g. the Independent Committee of Inquiry into Student Finance consultation process report entitled *Student Finance: fairness for the future*, SE/1999/58). All Laid Papers are listed in the Scottish Parliament publication, *Scottish Parliamentary and Statutory Publications.*

Policy position papers and consultation documents are an extremely important part of the whole process of government and legislation. As stated in Chapter 1, Bills presented to Parliament by the Executive are not the first stage in the parliamentary legislative process. Public consultation can take place for a considerable period prior to the preparation of a draft Bill. The publication of policy and consultation papers is frequently a signal of intended legislation and is designed to engender discussion and submission of opinion by interested parties. As an example of the way in which policy proceeds to legislation, figure 3 *(over)* shows the route from discussion paper to the Royal Assent of the **Adults with Incapacity (Scotland) Act**.

Fig. 3 From Policy to Legislation - Adults with Incapacity - For further detail

Scottish Executive Adults with Incapacity web-site (http://www.scotland.gov.u

1991	1995	1997	1999	Oct 1999
Scottish Law Commission Discussion Paper	Scottish Law Commission Report	Scottish Office Consultation Paper	SE Paper	Scottish Parliament Bill [As Introduced]
Mentally Disabled Adults - Legal Arrangements for Managing their Welfare and Finances	Report on Incapable Adults	Managing the Finances and Welfare of Incapable Adults	Making the Right Moves - Rights and protection for adults with incapacity	Adults with Incapacity (Scotland) Bill Published with: Explanatory and Policy Memoranda
Scottish Law Commission Discussion Paper No. 94	**Scottish Law Commission Report No. 151**		**SE/1999/24**	**SP Bill 5 SP Bill 5EN SP Bill 5PM**

The Bill was fully debated and the reports of the debates can be accessed through the Official Report on the Scottish Parliament Web-site.

See Also Scottish Parliament Information Centre (SPICe) Publications:

Research Note 99/07   **Adults with incapacity**

Research Note 99/14   **Adults with Incapacity (Scotland) Bill**

Research Note 99/47   **Adults with Incapacity (Scotland) Bill Part 5: Medical Treatment, Care and Research**

Research Notes 00/03   **Adults with Incapacity (Scotland) Bill (as amended at Stage 2)**

Research Note 00/12   **Adults with Incapacity (Scotland) Bill: the International Protection of Adults**

Research Note 00/22   **Adults with Incapacity (Scotland) Bill [as amended at Stage 2] Part 5: medical treatment and research**

Dec 1999	March 2000	March 2000	May 2000
Scottish Parliament Justice and Home Affairs Committee (Lead Committee)	Scottish Parliament Bill [As Amended at Stage 2]	Scottish Parliament Bill [As Passed]	Royal Assent
Stage 1 Report on the Adults with Incapacity (Scotland) Bill and Evidence	Adults with Incapacity (Scotland) Bill	Adults with Incapacity (Scotland) Bill	Adults with Incapacity (Scotland) Act
SPP 41 Session 1 (1999)	SP Bill 5A	SP Bill 5B	2000 asp 4

Central Research Unit (CRU) Publications

The Scottish Executive Central Research Unit (CRU) provides a research service to the whole Scottish Executive and certain allied Departments, such as the Crown Office and Procurator Fiscal Service. Its major concern is with research in relation to social policy but also covers areas such as transport, housing, social inclusion, rural affairs, children and young people, education, community care, local government, civil justice, regeneration, planning, women's issues and environmental matters. Although the final decision rests with the Scottish Ministers, the bulk of CRU commissioned research is published, usually as a series of Findings (brief summaries available free of charge) and full Reports. The summary findings are arranged into numbered series within generic groups (e.g. Social Work Research Findings, Legal Studies Research findings). Many of the full reports are available in full text on-line and a complete catalogue of the current state of publications, arranged chronologically, is available on the **Research Publications** (http://www.scotland.gov.uk/cru/pub.asp) page of the CRU web-site.

The research itself covers a wide range of topics investigating key contemporary issues (e.g. *Resolving Neighbour Disputes through Mediation in Scotland, Drug Misuse in Scotland, The Community Impact of Traffic Calming Schemes*) and includes commissioned literature and research reviews (e.g. *Literature Review of Social Exclusion*). The CRU also publishes the *Social Inclusion Research Bulletin*. Most CRU publications are available from The Stationery Office bookshops.

As stated earlier, individual Departments produce a variety of documents ranging from consultation papers, explanatory booklets and guides to detailed reports and statistical bulletins. Users should note that the Executive policy is increasingly to replace Statistical Bulletins with periodic news releases, on-line datasets and summary annual publications. For more detailed information about statistical material, see Chapter 7. The publications of each Department are recorded in the annual listing produced by SELIS. This listing also identifies material which is published by The Stationery Office and that published by the Executive itself (i.e. not by an individual Department). One other group of exceptions to the general rule of Departmental publishing is the reports of independent Committees of Inquiry, usually set up by a Scottish Minister (e.g. *A Teaching Profession for the 21st Century,* the report of the Committee of Inquiry into Professional Conditions of Service for Teachers, chaired by Gavin McCrone). Like their Westminster predecessors, such committee reports are frequently referred to by the name of the chairman. Major inquiries have their own web-sites as a central location for all information on membership, deliberations, evidence and reports (see below).

While it is true that Scottish Executive publications were initially difficult to trace, identify and obtain, SELIS does now indicate SE series numbers for documents published by the Executive.

The **Scottish Executive web-site** (http://www.scotland.gov.uk) should be the first and principal location to search when looking for material published by any of the Executive Departments, specialist units, advisory committees or working groups. Individual Departments are responsible for the structure of their section of the web-site and this leads to certain inconsistencies when searching. Users have three alternative ways in which to search the web-site for published material:

▶ Using the Publications page – possibly most valuable for recent publications,
▶ Searching under the publications of the individual Department – but this relies on knowing the responsible Department,
▶ Using the Search Engine (see below).

The web-site currently holds full-text publications from 1997 onwards and, from 2001, all publications are available in both HTML and PDF formats. Older publications are listed under **What We Do** (http://www.scotland.gov.uk/what.asp), sub-divided by category, or listed in alphabetical order in the Publications Archive. Readers should note that there can be differences between the formats in such matters as the inclusion of graphics or tables. A major problem with the web version has been that it provides few bibliographic details, ISBNs or prices for paper versions. As with many other sites, there has also been the difficulty of web addresses changing over time.

© Crown copyright

The home page of the site includes links to selected recent publications, latest headlines and that day's press releases. The latter are also accessible under:

▶ **News**
(http://www.scotland.gov.uk/news2/current.asp)

This link provides a daily listing for the last seven days with a calendar to allow archive searching. Such a facility can be invaluable when searching for information which may be poorly cited in the press. The press releases archive goes back to October 1997 and, therefore, pre-dates the establishment of the Scottish Executive. Occasionally, other Scottish Office material can be found on the different sections of the web-site.

▶ **Publications**
(http://www.scotland.gov.uk/publications/recent.asp)

The publications page is updated daily and provides links to documents issued within the last month. There are links to publications on external web-sites and pdf versions are noted. The page also provides a **Note on Scottish Executive Publications** (http://www.scotland.gov.uk/publications/note.asp), giving details of Crown copyright, finding a publication and bibliographic control. Publications can also be searched over a range of years by using the alphabetical sequence at the head of the page. Such a search produces a list of publications, regardless of subject, where the title begins with the selected letter. Other choices from the header include links to Bills, Scottish and UK Legislation, Consultations (see below) and Catalogue by Topic (see below).

The complete electronic archive of publications can also be searched by selecting the 'Catalogue by Topic' icon on the header. This retrieves 13 major category topics which in turn have sub-categories, which can be further sub-divided. Click on the category or sub-category of your choice and this will produce a list of direct links to relevant publications arranged in reverse chronological order. When searching by Topic, the category search string is displayed and allows users to return to a higher category.

▶ **Your Views**
(http://www.scotland.gov.uk/views/views.asp)

The section 'Your Views' links to current Consultations and provides a list of issued documents for public comment. This is different from the list accessed through the Publications section. Under 'Your Views', only those consultations open for comment (or where the closing date has just passed) are listed. In addition, consultations are added to the top of the list as they are published on the web-site. By going through the **Consultations** (http://www.scotland.gov.uk/views/consult.asp) route, the consultations are arranged by topic in an archive list. Both routes link to the same draft legislation and discussion forum pages.

▶ **Who We Are**
(http://www.scotland.gov.uk/who/who.asp)

Under the section **Who We Are**, there are links to the individual Departments and Agencies usually with a description of the responsibilities of the individual Department. This page also links to information about the **Scottish Ministers** and their responsibilities (http://www.scotland.gov.uk/who/ministers.asp), the **senior management** of the Executive Departments (http://www.scotland.gov.uk/who/senior.asp) and a short list of significant events in the history of the Executive. At the time of writing, only the **Enterprise and Lifelong Learning Department** has a separate home page section (http://www.scotland.gov.uk/who/elld) on the Scottish Executive web-site, with further information on its activities. This is designed with a menu at the left and links to such features as its **Innovation Bulletin** (http://www.scotland.gov.uk/who/elld/innovation1.asp), **research programme** (http://www.scotland.gov.uk/who/elld/res_tracker0.asp) and **statistics** (http://www.scotland.gov.uk/who/elld/stats.asp). It also supplies information on grant schemes and application forms, links to various consultations and working groups, and news flashes. Readers should also note that the Scottish Executive Environment and Rural Affairs Department has an **Agriculture** page (http://www.scotland.gov.uk/agri/) which brings together topics of particular interest to the Scottish agricultural and livestock industries. In addition, the **Health Department's** site is hosted by SHOW (Scottish Health on the Web) (http://www.show.scot.nhs.uk/sehd/) with no link from the Executive Departmental web-page at the time of writing.

▶ **What We Do**
(http://www.scotland.gov.uk/what.asp)

The section **What We Do** links to a drop-down menu selection of topics and special interest areas. By selecting an individual topic, users are linked to that topic's section of the Executive web-site where the responsible minister is usually named. For certain policy issues (e.g. European matters), there is no single responsible minister. Within topics, there are links to relevant special interest areas of the Executive web-site, press releases, contacts and other relevant external publications and web-sites.

It is very important for users to remember that topic and special interest areas are the only means to enter many of the significant policy making sections of the Executive web-site. Most of these topic sites are sub-divided and can be accessed via a menu on the left-hand side of the page. A bar at the top of the page provides links to higher level areas of the site and, where one exists, a site map can be valuable for gaining an overview of the topic site. For an example, see **Human Rights** (http://www.scotland.gov.uk/justice/humanrights/).

Not every topic has its own site and sites vary according to topic. For example, the Social Justice area of the web-site (http://www.scotland.gov.uk/socialjustice/ index.htm) is divided into sections on:

- **strategy** (http://www.scotland.gov.uk/socialjustice/strategy/index.htm), which provides information about the strategic aspects for social inclusion in Scotland. Specific areas can be accessed through links to milestones and targets, the annual report, and the Scottish Social Inclusion Network,

- **delivery** (http://www.scotland.gov.uk/socialjustice/delivery/index.htm), the main operational area of this section, carrying current and background details about many social justice initiatives. These include Social Inclusion Partnerships, with links to individual partnership sites, and the Working for Communities programme and its pathfinder pages,

- **publications** (http://www.scotland.gov.uk/socialjustice/publications/ index.htm) linking to a range of relevant documents,

- **research** (http://www.scotland.gov.uk/socialjustice/research/index.htm) linking to relevant research projects and documents,

- **contacts** (http://www.scotland.gov.uk/socialjustice/contacts.htm) which provides a quick route to the contact information to be found in different areas of the site.

There are also sections to other links and a search option taking the user back to the Executive search engine.

Other sites (e.g. **Climate Change in Scotland** (http://www.scotland.gov.uk/ climatechange)) concentrate more on background information, questions and answers, publications and news releases. The design of the various topic sections can differ according to topic. The **Homelessness Task force web-site** (http://www.scotland. gov.uk/homelessness) has a design markedly similar to that of the Executive and links to its reports, the research sub-group and the work of the electronic data capture project board are found at the end of the introduction.

Committees of Inquiry, Consultation and Initiative Web-sites

Nowhere is the access to information through topic pages more important than those created for Committees of Inquiry, Consultations and the various policy initiatives inaugurated by the Executive. One such initiative is **Digital Scotland** (http://www.scotland.gov.uk/digitalscotland), which aims to ensure the maximum economic and social advantage for Scotland from information and communication technologies. It can be traced directly through the special interest areas of the site map. Related initiatives identified on the **Digital Scotland** web page (e.g. **21st century government for Scotland** (http://www.scotland.gov.uk/government/c21g/default.asp)

are not always easy to find and are only accessible through other links, in this case under the topic heading **Government** (http://www.scotland.gov.uk/whatwedo.asp?topic= government). More difficult to trace can be web-sites created for consultation purposes (e.g. Scottish Executive **Alcohol Misuse Web-site** (http://www.scotland.gov.uk/health/ alcoholmisuse) which is not listed under the Health topic or under the special interest areas. It can be traced by using the Executive search engine for a simple search using the term 'alcohol misuse web-site' but without a clear guide to these various sites, users are reliant on their own knowledge of what might be available.

On occasion, the Executive may set up an independent Committee of Inquiry (e.g. **Independent Committee of Inquiry into Student Finance** (Cubie Committee) (http://www.studentfinance.org.uk)) or Commission (e.g. **Scottish Charity Law Review Commission** (McFadden Committee) (http://www.charityreview.com)) to investigate a particular aspect of devolved responsibility. When this occurs, a web-site may be created to provide information about the workings and process of the Committee, the terms of reference, Committee papers, news releases and contact details as well as links to other relevant sites with useful background information. Final reports can also be available here. Once again, users may have to rely on press releases or other sources for guidance on what is available.

Searching the Scottish Executive Web-site
(http://www.scotland.gov.uk/search2/search.asp)

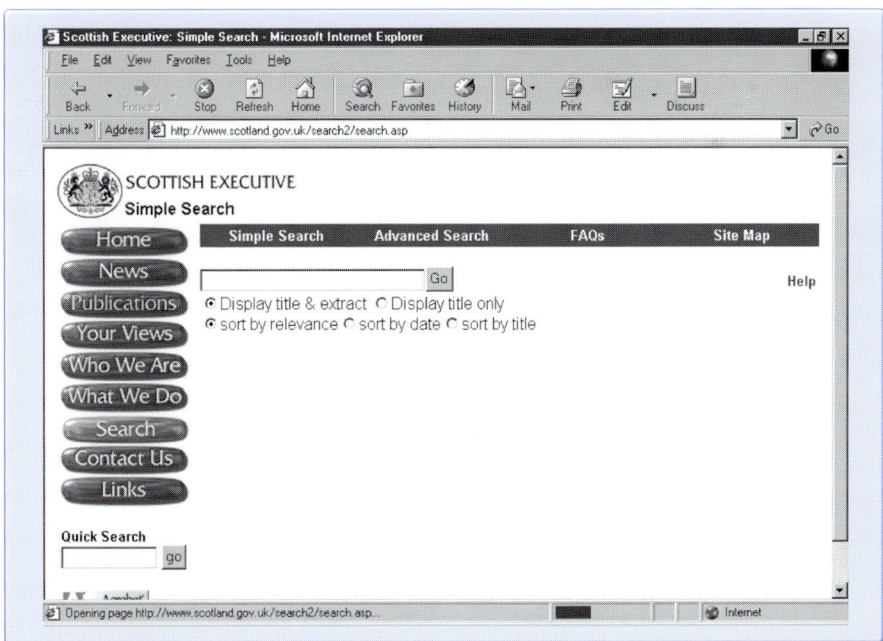

The Executive web-site can be searched using its own Search engine. This page is divided into four sections – **simple search** (http://www.scotland.gov.uk/search2/search.asp), **advanced search** (http://www.scotland.gov.uk/search2/advsearch.asp), **frequently asked questions (FAQs)** (http://www.scotland.gov.uk/faq/faq.asp), and **site map** (http://www.scotland.gov.uk/search2/site.asp). Only the simple search option allows searching for words within the text of a document and this option allows the choice of displaying either the title only or the title and an extract. The maximum number of results displayed is 200 but varying the search will produce different results. Only a very basic Boolean search, using 'AND' or 'OR' can be attempted and the engine does not accept searches using 'NOT'. Using 'AND' will return pages where all the words appear. Phrase searching should be kept to a minimum (e.g. nursery education, livestock farming). Where several terms or extended phrase searching is attempted, this frequently produces no results (e.g. child drug abuse). Results can be sorted by relevance, by date or by title. A key to the type of file (e.g. web page or plain text file, Adobe Acrobat file or Microsoft Word document) is displayed with the results. While search tips are provided under 'Help', this concentrates on search phrases and document types more than on the results.

The **advanced search option** (http://www.scotland.gov.uk/search2/advsearch.asp) is a more useful tool for users seeking to concentrate on specific material as it allows searching by category, date and type (i.e. publications, Central Research Unit, news releases, statistical). There are 29 categories ranging from agriculture to transport and including enterprise, food, heritage and sport. Results can be sorted into reverse chronological or alphabetical order and searching can be done on exact phrase, all or any words. It is important to remember that the advanced search option only searches the titles of documents.

Frequently asked questions (FAQs) (http://www.scotland.gov.uk/faq/faq.asp) appears as a reactive service providing answers to specific enquiries on a wide range of issues. The answers are arranged alphabetically by topic and provide the kind of direct information required. Coverage of topics is clearly based on the questions asked and there are some notable gaps in matters discussed.

The **site map** (http://www.scotland.gov.uk/search2/site.asp) is a useful means of finding one's way through the Executive web-site. It lists the various sub-sections by heading and allows direct access to individual topic and special interest areas.

▶ **Contact Us**
   (http://www.scotland.gov.uk/contact/address.asp)

   This section of the web-site provides users with information on the addresses and contact telephone numbers for the Executive Departments. It also allows users the opportunity to provide feedback to the Executive, either on the quality of service from its staff or on any aspect of its web-site. Users can complete a prepared template to ask questions or complain about any aspect of service. The charters of individual public bodies are listed and each should indicate the action to be taken when complaining.

▶ Links
(http://www.scotland.gov.uk/links.asp)

Finally, the Executive web-site provides a list of links to other relevant sites under twelve categories – education, Europe, health, industry, miscellaneous, other Scottish web-sites, parliaments, Scottish government and public bodies, Scottish local government, tourism, traffic, travel and transport and UK government. The links are arranged alphabetically.

Other Relevant Publications

Office of the Queen's Printer for Scotland

Apart from Scottish Statutory Instruments, which are printed under the authority and superintendence of the Queen's Printer for Scotland, this office is also responsible for publishing the *Edinburgh Gazette*.

Edinburgh Gazette

Registered as a newspaper, the *Edinburgh Gazette* appears twice weekly on Tuesdays and Fridays and is a record of a wide variety of public information. In particular, it provides details of corporate and personal insolvency, and changes in company regulations and partnerships. Revocations of Acts and orders, planning applications covering listed buildings, oil exploration licenses, prohibition orders of road traffic acts, changes in the cost of postage and National Savings rates, notifications of Royal Assent, honours, regius professorships and appointments to public bodies are also included. Under the section Health, details of product licenses granted for, for example prescription only medicines, are given. A Company Law Official Notifications Supplement is issued on the same days (with separate page numbering) and this gives information on new companies, changes to directors, the delivery of annual accounts and such matters. Neither sequence has a contents page or index. The format of the Gazette changed with the establishment of the Scottish Parliament.

Scotland Forum

Scotland Forum was a monthly newsletter of sixteen issues that focussed on issues relating to the new parliament and government in Scotland. It appeared soon after the publication of the Scotland Bill in January 1988 and included articles on various aspects of devolved matters, in addition to listings of Scottish Office press releases, Scottish official publications and a selective bibliography of items about the Scottish Parliament.

Legal and Judicial Information

T he principal aim of this chapter is to introduce users to the main sources of 'official' information, both printed and electronic, available on the Scottish legal system. This chapter does not attempt to include the 'non-official' sources of legal information, such as the commercially produced Law Reports series or the electronic databases widely used by practitioners and academics. It concentrates on those public bodies and organisations producing publications, or public information, on some aspect of the Scottish legal system on a regular or occasional basis. The law of the European Union, which is, of course, part of the law of Scotland, will be discussed in detail in Chapter 5. The publications of the Court of Justice, however, will be discussed here under Courts.

Scottish Parliament

The **Scotland Act 1998** (http://www.legislation.hmso.gov.uk/acts/acts1998/ 19980046.htm) devolved extensive law-making powers to the Scottish Parliament. The Parliament is able to make primary legislation ('Acts of the Scottish Parliament') in certain areas, known as 'devolved' matters, which include most aspects of the criminal and civil law, criminal justice and the prosecution system, and the courts. The legislative function and processes of the Scottish Parliament are discussed in detail in Chapter 1.

It is important to note that the Parliament's two Justice Committees (which both have remits 'to consider and report on matters relating to the administration of civil and criminal justice, the reform of the civil and criminal law and such other matters as fall within the responsibility of the Minister for Justice)' are the principal Parliamentary bodies looking at civil and criminal justice matters.

Both **Justice 1** (http://www.scottish.parliament.uk/official_report/cttee/just1.htm) and **Justice 2** (http://www.scottish.parliament.uk/official_report/cttee/just2.htm) produce Official Reports, Agenda and Minutes of Proceedings (available only electronically) and Reports (which are issued as SP Papers). Please note that before 2001, civil and criminal justice matters were the responsibility of the Justice and Home Affairs Committee and its papers and reports are archived on the Scottish Parliament web-site: **1999 papers** (http://www.scottish.parliament.uk/official_report/cttee/archive/just-99.htm#off) **2000 papers** (http://www.scottish.parliament.uk/official_report/cttee/archive/just-00.htm#pap).

Another important Scottish Parliament Committee in the legislative context is, of course, the **Subordinate Legislation Committee** (http://www.scottish.parliament.uk/ official_report/cttee/subord.htm) whose task is to scrutinise Scottish Statutory Instruments (SSIs) and subordinate legislation in bills. For more detail on the publishing output of Scottish Parliament Committees, both printed and electronic, see Chapter 1.

The Scottish Parliament Information Centre (SPICe) has produced a very useful Subject Map, **Sources of Scots Law** (http://www.scottish.parliament.uk/whats_happening/ research/pdf_subj_maps/smda-04.pdf) which provides a basic outline of the sources of Scots Law. Please note that this document only appears on the web.

Scottish Executive

The Scottish Executive Justice Department (SEJD) is responsible for aspects of criminal justice policy and procedure, civil law matters, such as matrimonial and family law, policy on victims of crime and regulation of charities. It also has responsibilities for the legal aid system in Scotland and aspects of the work of district courts. The Executive supports the operations of a number of courts and tribunals such as the Scottish Land Court and the VAT and Duties Tribunal and also has a role in administering the system of appointments of the Judiciary in Scotland (other than appointments to the District Courts). In addition to these functions it is also responsible for the police and fire services in Scotland and criminal justice social work.

The **Justice Department** (http://www.scotland.gov.uk/whatwedo.asp?topic=justice) section of the Scottish Executive web-site has links to all **documents** (http://www.scotland. gov.uk/whatwedo.asp?type=pub&topic=justice) published under their auspices or from associated Executive Agencies and non-departmental public bodies. The Department's **Press Releases** (http://www.scotland.gov.uk/whatwedo.asp?type=press&topic=justice) is a very useful source of information for users who need to keep up to date with current developments.

Courts

Scottish Courts

Two bodies, The Scottish Courts Group and The Scottish Courts Service, both of which are Executive Agencies and part of the Scottish Executive Justice Department, administer the Scottish Courts. The Scottish Courts Group is, broadly speaking, responsible for the effective administration of justice in Scotland. This includes the administration of judicial appointments, dealing with complaints against the judiciary and responsibility for the development of policy for civil justice in Scotland and private international law. The Courts Group also finance the operations a number of courts and tribunals such as the Scottish Land Court and the VAT and Duties Tribunal. The Scottish Courts Service is responsible for the administration of the Supreme and Sheriff Courts.

The Supreme Courts of Scotland consist of the Court of Session, the High Court of Justiciary and the Accountant of the Court's Office. The **Court of Session** (http://www.scotcourts.gov.uk/session/session.htm) is the supreme civil court in Scotland and is situated at Parliament House in Edinburgh. The **High Court of Justiciary** (http://www.scotcourts.gov.uk/justiciary/justiciary.htm) deals with criminal appeals and serious criminal cases. Although the Court is based in Edinburgh, trials are held in towns and cities throughout Scotland as a means of reducing inconvenience to witnesses, jurors and court users. The Accountant of the Court's Office is responsible for the supervision of individuals who have been appointed by the Courts to look after the property of persons unable to do so themselves.

The lower court in Scotland is the **Sheriff Court** (http://www.scotcourts.gov.uk/html/ sheriff.htm). Each Sheriffdom (of which there are six) has a Sheriff Principal, with Sheriffs sitting in each main town. This court has both civil and criminal jurisdictions. The court dealing with petty criminal matters is the District Court. Each local authority district has a Magistrates Court. The Magistrate may be a lay justice sitting with an assessor or a stipendiary magistrate who is legally qualified. Please note that the Scottish Courts Group and Scottish Court Service have no responsibility for the operations of the District Courts. They are managed individually by each Local Authority.

Scottish Courts web-site
(http://www.scotcourts.gov.uk/)

The **Scottish Court web-site** (http://www.scotcourts.gov.uk/) provides an access point to information relating to all civil and criminal courts within Scotland, including the Court of Session, the High Court of Justiciary, the Sheriff Courts and a number of other courts, commissions and tribunals, as well the District Courts.

The opinions of both the Supreme Courts and the Sheriff Courts are available on the **Scottish Courts web-site** (http://www.scotcourts.gov.uk/). There are however, two separate search engines provided for locating cases; one for the **Supreme Courts** (http://www.scotcourts.gov.uk/pages/supreme_opinions.htm) and the other for the **Sheriff Courts** (http://www.scotcourts.gov.uk/pages/sheriff_opinions.htm). It is important to note that a **Keyword Search** (http://www.muscat.com/cgi-bin/empower. scottishcourts?DB=scottishcourts) will search **ALL** cases on the web-site, including cases for the Court of Session and High Court as well as the Sheriff Courts.

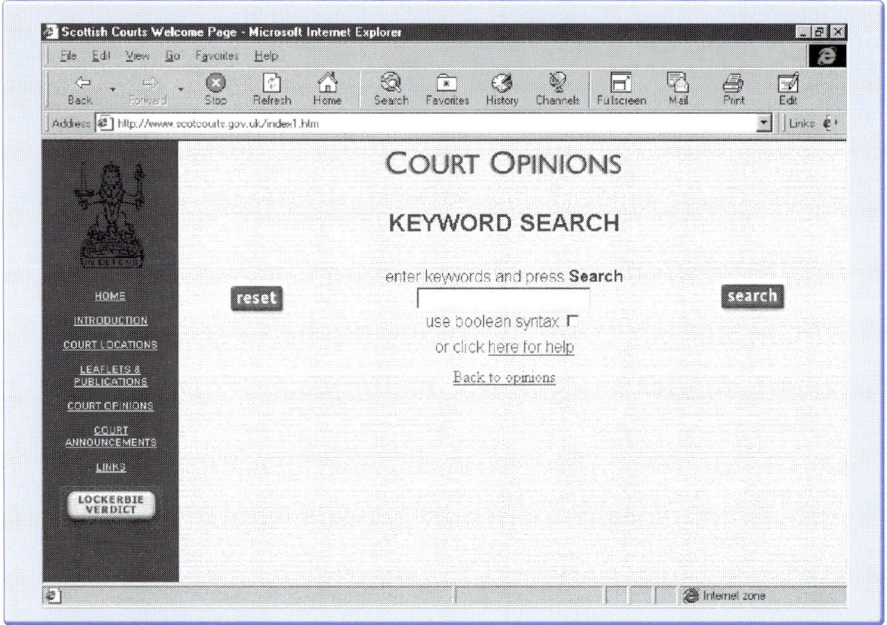

Court of Session opinions are available from September 1998 (note that opinions in commercial cases are available from January 1998). Criminal opinions of the High Court of Justiciary, including opinions in some sentence appeals, are available. Sheriff Court opinions are available from September 1998 but note that not all cases coming before the Sheriff Courts will be reported on the site. Only where there is a **significant** point of law or **particular** public interest will the details be published.

The search engine interface is the same for both Courts. You can search by **Keyword** (http://www.muscat.com/cgi-bin/empower.scottishcourts?DB=scottishcourts), which will search the full text of all the judgements published on the Internet for the keywords that you enter. You can also use a structured search where you can search judgements by type, date, name of sheriff(s), pursuer/appellant, defender/respondent and type of action. You can view a list of the types of action that are available. Court Opinions are updated at approximately 2.00 p.m. on any day on which new opinions are to be published.

The **Scottish Courts** (http://www.scotcourts.gov.uk/) web-site does not host information for or about the District Courts. It does provide a link, however, to the **District Courts Association web-site** (http://www.district-courts.org.uk/), which provides information about the District Court system in Scotland, as well as court location details and contact numbers. At present it contains no Court opinions or judgements.

The **Scottish Court Service** (http://www.scotcourts.gov.uk/html/scservice.htm) and **Scottish Courts Group** (http://www.scotcourts.gov.uk/admin/scadmin.htm) also publish a number of leaflets and other documents relating to their work. These publications can be obtained from the Scottish Court Service Headquarters or Scottish Executive Justice Department, Courts Group. Alternatively, they can be downloaded from the **Publications and Leaflets** (http://www.scotcourts.gov.uk/html/guidance.htm section of the web-site.

UK Courts with a Scottish Jurisdiction

House of Lords

The House of Lords is the final court of appeal on points of law in civil cases for the whole of the United Kingdom. Therefore, it hears appeals from the Court of Session in Scotland, as well as appeals on criminal cases for England, Wales and Northern Ireland.

The full text of all Opinions delivered since 14 November 1996 are available on the **Judicial Business section of the House of Lords web-site** (http://www.parliament.the-stationery-office.co.uk/pa/ld199697/ldjudgmt/ldjudgmt.htm). The judgements appear in reverse chronological order. The text of Opinions appears on this site within 2 hours of their delivery in the House. Paper copies are available from the Judicial Office.

Privy Council Judicial Committee

The Privy Council Judicial Committee has jurisdiction to hear and determine questions relating to the competences and functions of the legislative and executive authorities established in Scotland and Northern Ireland by the Scotland Act 1998 and the Northern Ireland Act 1998, respectively, and questions as to the competence and functions of the Assembly established by the Government of Wales Act 1998.

The full text of judgements in devolution cases are available on the **Privy Council Judicial Committee web-site** (http://www.privy-council.org.uk/judicial-committee/ jindex.htm). Judgements are arranged annually, with a separate web page for each year from 1999 onwards. Judgements in devolution cases are separately listed at the bottom of each web page. Please note that items in italic indicate that the judgement is an advance copy, still subject to minor amendments.

Other Courts

Court of Justice and Court of First Instance

The Court of Justice of the European Communities is made up of fifteen judges assisted by nine advocates-general appointed for six years by agreement among the Member States. The Court of Justice ensures that Community law is uniformly interpreted and effectively applied. It has jurisdiction in disputes involving Member States, EU institutions, businesses and individuals. The Court is assisted by a Court of First Instance, set up in 1989, which has special responsibility for dealing with administrative disputes in the European institutions and disputes arising from the Community competition rules. The major printed publication of the Court of Justice is *Reports of Cases Before the Court of Justice and the Court of First Instance*, commonly know as *European Court Reports* published in Luxembourg by the Office for Official Publications of the European Communities. Since 1989, the Reports have been published in two sections. Section I covers cases before the Court of Justice and Section II cases before the Court of First Instance. The time lag between the delivery of the judgements and their publication in print is approximately six months. They are the **only** authentic source for citations of decisions of the European Courts.

Court of Justice and Court of First Instance web-site
(http://curia.eu.int/en/index.htm)

The full text of all judgements, opinions and orders delivered by the Court since June 1997 are available in the **Recent Case Law** (http://curia.eu.int/jurisp/cgi-bin/form.pl?lang=en) section of the **Court** (http://curia.eu.int/en/index.htm) web-site (excluding Court of First Instance on staff cases). Users can search by case number, party, or by words in text. Check the appropriate type in the 'document required option' at the top left of the search box (see below). Please note that the 'document required option' automatically defaults to an 'all documents' option.

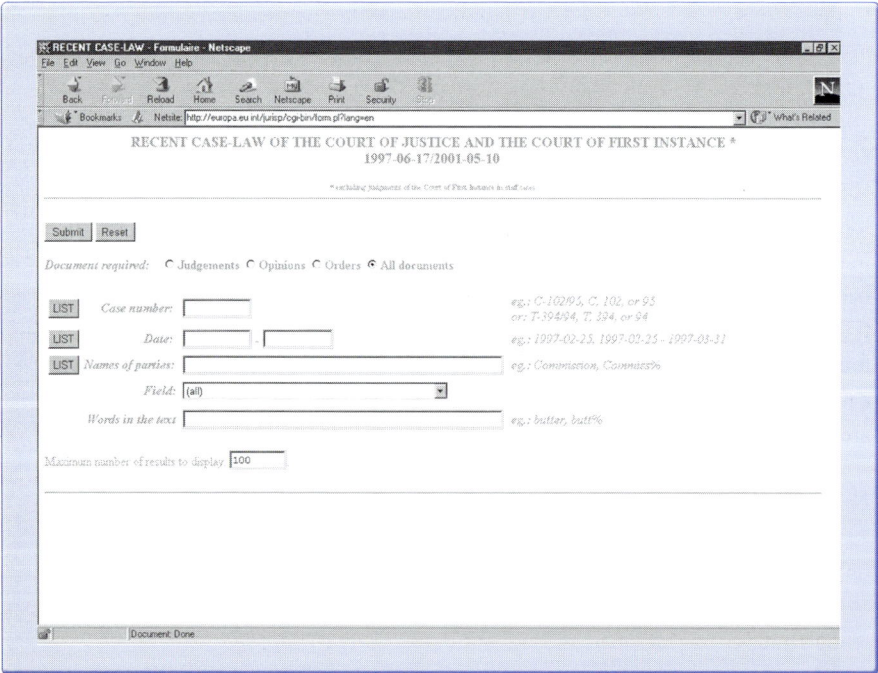

© European Communities, 1995-2001

The **Research and Documentation** (http://europa.eu.int/cj/en/recdoc/index.htm) section of the web-site contains other useful databases although some of these are only available in French at the time of writing. These include:

▶ **Digest of Community Case Law** (http://europa.eu.int/cj/en/recdoc/repert/index.htm) - Summaries of judgements and orders of the Court of Justice and the Court of First Instance arranged according to subject-matter,

▶ **Alphabetical index of subject-matter** (http://europa.eu.int/cj/en/recdoc/tabmat/index.htm) - Alphabetical index of legal issues addressed by the case law of the Court of Justice and the Court of First Instance and the Opinions of Advocates General. This is available in English from 1991-1998.

The **Press Releases-Cases** (http://europa.eu.int/cj/en/cp/aff/index.htm) section is also useful for finding information on very recent important judgements or opinions. Another source of up-to-date information is the *Proceedings of the European Court of Justice* (chiefly summaries of judgements) - a weekly bulletin which can be found on the **RAPID** (http://europa.eu.int/rapid/start/welcome.html) database on the **European Commission** (http://europa.eu.int/) web-site.

European Court of Human Rights

The European Court of Human Rights is an institution of the Council of Europe. The Council of Europe should not be confused with the European Union. The two organisations are quite distinct. The 15 European Union states, however, are all members of the Council of Europe. The Convention for the Protection of Human Rights and Fundamental Freedoms (http://conventions.coe.int/treaty/EN/WhatYouWant.asp?NT=005&CM=8&DF=11/06/01), more commonly known as The European Convention on Human Rights, was drawn up within the Council of Europe in 1950 and entered into force in September 1953. The Convention is unusual amongst international Conventions in having enforcement mechanisms including a court. Since 1966, British citizens have had the right to apply to the European Commission of Human Rights if they feel that their rights under the Convention have been infringed by the State. If the Commission found an application admissible and meritorious, it could refer the case to the Court for a judgement. From November 1998, the Commission ceased to exist and applications are now made directly to the Court.

Under the terms of the **Scotland Act 1998** (http://www.hmso.gov.uk/acts/acts1998/19980046.htm), the Scottish Executive and the Scottish Parliament, in exercising their powers, are required to comply with those rights set out in the European Convention on Human Rights. These requirements were extended to all public authorities (e.g. NHS, schools and local authorities) throughout the United Kingdom by the **Human Rights Act 1998** (http://www.hmso.gov.uk/acts/acts1998/19980042.htm). Both the Westminster and Scottish Parliaments must consider the human rights aspects of every Bill. Judges must take account of the Convention in deciding cases, and for the first time, individuals who consider that their Convention rights have been infringed have the right to seek redress in Scottish courts. For more information on human rights in Scotland, see the **Scottish Executive Human Rights web-site** (http://www.scotland.gov.uk/justice/humanrights/default.asp).

European Court of Human Rights web-site
(http://www.echr.coe.int)

The full text of all judgements delivered by the Court are on the **HUDOC** database (http://www.echr.coe.int/Hudoc.htm) available on the Court's web-site. Searching on HUDOC is relatively straightforward.

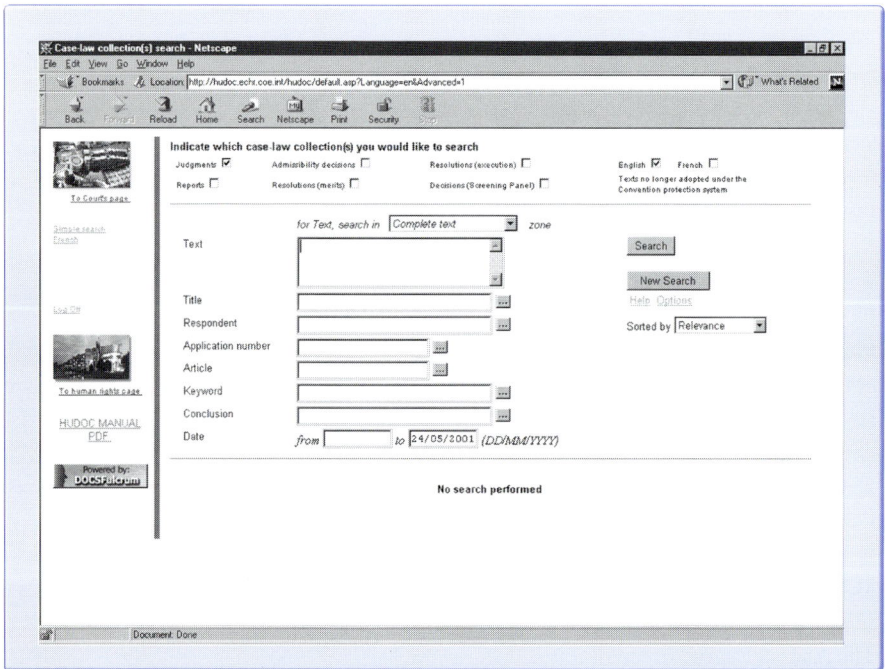

© European Court of Human Rights

At the top of the screen, users can choose what case law collection to search. Note that the automatic default is 'Judgements'. Search criteria can be entered into one or several fields (e.g. text, title, application number). Please note that the text search option is extremely sophisticated. HUDOC can search within the text of a document for whole sentences, phrases and words. The whole range of Boolean operators (AND, OR, NOT, proximity, precedence, and multiple and single wildcard(s)) are available. The 'sorted by' box on the far right of the screen allows users to select the way that results will be displayed. The default setting is 'Relevance' but 'Date' (both chronological and reverse chronological), 'Title' (alphabetical), 'Respondent' and 'Application number' are also available. For more information on how to search HUDOC efficiently and effectively, use the **HUDOC manual** (http://www.echr.coe.int/Eng/Edocs/HudocManualEng.pdf) which is available (in pdf format) on the web-site by clicking on the icon on the navigation bar on the left of the screen.

The **List of Recent Judgements** (http://hudoc.echr.coe.int/hudoc/default.asp?Language= en&Cmd=Query&Tname=Hejud&appno=all&RelatedMode=1) and **Press Releases** (http://www.echr.coe.int/Eng/Press/PressReleases.htm) sections of the web-site are also useful for finding information on very recent important judgements or opinions.

Scottish Legal Bodies and Organisations

Crown Office and **Procurator Fiscal Service**
(www.crownoffice.gov.uk) and (www.procuratorfiscal.gov.uk)

The Crown Office and Procurator Fiscal Service provides Scotland's independent public prosecution and deaths investigation service. It is a Department of the Scottish Executive and is headed by the Lord Advocate. The Department is the sole public prosecution authority in Scotland. It is responsible for making decisions about, and bringing prosecutions for, almost all criminal offences and the investigation of all sudden, suspicious or unexplained deaths. The Department is also responsible for deciding whether criminal proceedings or a Fatal Accident Inquiry should be held and for conducting such proceedings and inquiries.

The Crown Office (www.crownoffice.gov.uk) and **Procurator Fiscal Service** (www.procuratorfiscal.gov.uk) share two addresses and both will allow access to the one web-site. The Department produces a range of publications and leaflets with summaries and/or full text of published documents available on the **Information** (http://www.crownoffice.gov.uk/publications/newpublics.htm) section of the web-site. The **Annual Report** (http://www.crownoffice.gov.uk/departmental/99-2000%20Annual %20Report/index.html) is available in pdf format.

The Law Society of Scotland
(http://www.lawscot.org.uk/)

The Law Society of Scotland is the governing body for Scottish solicitors. The main publication of the Society is the *Journal of the Law Society of Scotland (JLSS)* which is the professional journal of solicitors in Scotland and is published monthly. The Society also produces a wide range of printed documents covering a broad range of legal topics, including easy-to-understand leaflets giving information on a broad range of legal topics. The full range of **publications and leaflets** (http://www.lawscot.org.uk/public/publicat.html) produced by the **Law Society** (http://www.lawscot.org.uk/) is available on their web-site in pdf format. The Law Society also publishes one of Scotland's principle legal directories know as the *Blue Book*. The *Blue Book* provides alphabetical and geographical listings of advocates, solicitors and legal firms, as well as information about courts, government departments and other legal organisations. The Law Society makes much of this information available on their web-site through searchable directories under the following categories:

▶ **Solicitors** (http://www.lawscot.org.uk/all.html) - search by forename and/or surname, the firm or geographical location.

▶ **Firms and Branches** (http://www.lawscot.org.uk/scripts/firms.asp) - search by the firm name, geographical location or by category of work undertaken.

▶ **Organisations with solicitors** (http://www.lawscot.org.uk/scripts/firms_nl.asp) - organisations, other than legal firms, which employ solicitors. Search by organisation name and its geographical location.

▶ **Accredited Specialists** (http://www.lawscot.org.uk/accredit.html) - search by forename and/or surname, the firm name, geographical location or specialism.

They also host a very useful suite of web pages called **What is Scots Law** (http://www.lawscot.org.uk/whatis/whatis_frame.html) which provides an easy-to-understand overview of the Scottish legal system. It has links to pages on the **History of Scots Law** (http://www.lawscot.org.uk/history/history.html) and the **Courts System** (http://www.lawscot.org.uk/whatis/courts.html). The web-site also includes the **Dial-a-Law** (http://www.lawscot.org.uk/dialalaw.html) service - the Law Society of Scotland's information and referral service. This service provides basic information on a range of different legal topics including family law, employment law, and crofting law.

Scottish Criminal Cases Review Commission
(http://www.sccrc.org.uk/).

The Scottish Criminal Cases Review Commission is a non-departmental public body with powers to consider alleged miscarriages of justice and to refer those meeting the relevant criteria back to the Criminal Appeal Court in Edinburgh for review. It is then up to the Court to decide if the conviction should be overturned. Decisions of cases referred back to the Courts are made available on the Scottish Courts Service web-site as they become available, although the **High Court** (http://www.sccrc.org.uk/highcourt.htm) section of the **Scottish Criminal Cases Review Commission web-site** (http://www.sccrc.org.uk/) provides a summary of the judgement as well as the reasons for referral from the Commission.

The major printed publication of the Commission is its **Annual Report** (http://www.sccrc.org.uk/ar/ccar-00.htm) which is also available in full text in both html and **pdf format** (http://www.sccrc.org.uk/forms/sccrcar1.pdf).

(http://www.scotlawcom.gov.uk/)

The Scottish Law Commission is an independent body established by the Law Commissions Act, 1965. The Commission's main task is to keep the law of Scotland under review and to recommend reforms when necessary. In this way the law is improved, brought up-to-date, made simpler and more accessible. Reform of the law itself must be done through Parliament and the Scottish Parliament. The Commission assists that reform by carrying out research and consultation so as to formulate proposals on a systematic basis for consideration.

The Commission's authority to carry out work is contained in a series of ongoing programmes of law reform approved by the Scottish Executive on the basis of a reference from them. At the time of writing, the Commission was currently working under the authority of the **Sixth Programme of Law Reform** (http://www.scotlawcom.gov.uk/report-6/page-1.htm) (Note that this publication was issued as an SE Paper (SE2000/27)). This publication set out the short, medium and long-term projects to be tackled by the Commission. The **Current Projects** (http://www.scotlawcom.gov.uk/html/current.htm) section of the **Commission web-site** (http://www.scotlawcom.gov.uk/) gives a brief outline of the projects currently being undertaken. **Annual Reports** (http://www.scotlawcom.gov.uk/html/annualreports.htm) indicate progress on each project.

For each project, the Commission prepares a **discussion paper** (http://www.scotlawcom.gov.uk/search/discussion.htm) setting out in detail the existing law and any defects, the arguments for and against possible solutions. The discussion paper is circulated widely to lawyers, relevant professional bodies and individuals, and others who are interested in that particular topic, and comments invited. Once the consultation process is complete, a **report** (http://www.scotlawcom.gov.uk/search/reports.htm) is prepared. This document sets out the conclusions of that process and gives the Commission's final recommendations. The report is submitted to the Scottish Executive as an SE Paper and, if the area in question is a matter reserved to the legislative competence of Parliament, the report will also be submitted to the Secretary of State for Scotland. If the report recommends a change in the law there will normally be a draft Bill attached to the report to demonstrate how the proposed reforms may be given effect.

Its major publications are:

▶ **Annual Reports** (http://www.scotlawcom.gov.uk/html/annualreports.htm) - the full text of the current annual report is available on the Scottish Law Commission web-site in pdf format. Note that annual reports are issued as SE Papers.

▶ **Discussion Papers** (http://www.scotlawcom.gov.uk/search/discussion.htm) - A complete listing of all discussion papers (or consultative memoranda as they were originally known) published from 1966 is available on the Scottish Law Commission web-site. Papers from 2000 (No. 110) are available in full text in pdf format. Discussion papers from no.112 onwards, can be purchased from The Stationery Office.

▶ **Programme of Law Reform** (http://www.scotlawcom.gov.uk/html/lawreform.htm) - Papers outlining the current programme available in full text in pdf format. Issued as SE Papers.

▶ **Reports** (http://www.scotlawcom.gov.uk/html/annualreports.htm) - a complete listing of all reports published since 1965 is available on the Scottish Law Commission web-site. Some reports from 1989 onwards are available in full text in pdf format. (See web-site for details). Note that reports are issued as SE Papers.

Scottish Legal Aid Board
(http://www.slab.org.uk/)

The Scottish Legal Aid Board is a non-departmental public body responsible for managing legal aid in Scotland. The main tasks of the Board are to deal with applications for legal aid, to pay solicitors and advocates for the legal aid work they do and to advise Scottish Ministers on legal aid matters. The Board produces a range of publications for the legal profession and the public. This includes the *Scottish Legal Aid Handbook* containing details of the legislation and regulations relating to legal aid.

The **publications** (http://www.slab.org.uk/contents/resources/publications/index.htm) section of the **Board web-site** (http://www.slab.org.uk/) provides details of all documents and leaflets produced by them. The **Annual Report** (http://www.slab.org.uk/contents/resources/Report.pdf) and **Corporate Plan** (http://www.slab.org.uk/contents/resources/Corpplan.pdf) are the only notable documents made available in full text, in pdf format.

Scottish Legal Services Ombudsman
(http://www.slso.org.uk/)

The Scottish Legal Services Ombudsman oversees the handling of complaints against legal practitioners. The Ombudsman is independent of both the legal profession and government and the Ombudsman's findings or recommendations are **not** subject to review by the Scottish Executive.

The Ombudsman publishes an **Annual Report** (http://www.slso.org.uk/reports.html), the most recent of which is available on the **Scottish Legal Services Ombudsman** (http://www.slso.org.uk/) web-site.

Advocate General for Scotland
(http://www.scottishsecretary.gov.uk/ags.htm)

With the creation of the Scottish Parliament, the Lord Advocate and the Solicitor General for Scotland transferred to the Scottish Executive. A new office, that of Advocate General for Scotland, was created to give opinions and provide informal advice to the UK Government, particularly in relation to Scots law. The Advocate General for Scotland has statutory functions under the Scotland Act 1998 and has overall responsibility for the work of the Legal Secretariat and of the Office of the Solicitor to the Advocate General, which provides legal services relating to Scotland to United Kingdom departments and agencies.

The Scotland Office web-site (http://www.scottishsecretary.gov.uk/) has a page providing a description of the office of Advocate General and contact information (http://www.scottishsecretary.gov.uk/ags.htm). The site also has a page of contact information for the Scotland Office (http://www.scottishsecretary.gov.uk/contact.htm) and links to other useful sites (http://www.scottishsecretary.gov.uk/links.htm). For more information on the work of the Scotland Office, see Chapter 4.

Chapter 4

Official Publications from Westminster relating to Scotland

T his chapter seeks to discuss Official Publications which relate to Scotland and emanate from the Westminster Parliament and its executive Departments and Offices. It is not intended to provide a detailed description of the publications of the United Kingdom Parliament and government, which are well described elsewhere. The chapter will not consider the legislative process in Parliament but it is very important for users to remember that much UK legislation continues to have a relevance and power in Scotland. In the discussion, a certain familiarity with the Westminster Parliament is assumed (e.g. knowledge of the existence of the two Houses).

No matter how the terms of the Scotland Act 1998 may have affected the constitutional position of Scotland within the wider United Kingdom, Westminster retains the supreme legislative authority and has the power to make laws for Scotland. The position of Secretary of State for Scotland, with a seat in the Cabinet, continues and carries responsibility for representing Scottish interests within the UK government on 'reserved' matters (see Introduction) and ensuring co-operation between the Scottish Parliament and Westminster. The Secretary of State heads the Scotland Office and it is through the Secretary of State that the UK Parliament allocates the Scottish Parliament's budget.

As stated, the UK Parliament retains responsibility for 'reserved' matters such as constitutional issues, defence, employment, foreign policy, immigration and nationality, and telecommunications. Legislation, and debate relating to these matters will continue to be at Westminster. Many Acts of the UK Parliament and much secondary legislation, again in the form of Statutory Instruments, will continue to have legislative power in Scotland. Users will need to remember to consider whether or not their area of interest is solely a 'devolved' or 'reserved' matter or a mixture of both.

Issues of state policy and concern in 'reserved' matters will continue to be investigated in Parliament. As an example of this, the Competition Commission investigated the supply of fresh processed milk to middle ground retailers in Scotland in 2000. The subsequent report, *Scottish Milk: a report on the supply of fresh processed milk to middle-ground retailers in Scotland*, was published as a Command Paper (Cm 5002) and presented to Parliament by the Secretary of State for Trade and Industry. Other issues of concern to all parts of the United Kingdom will continue to be debated at Westminster and it cannot be over-stressed that users must continue to be aware of the publications issued by Parliament and its executive bodies.

It should also be restated that the whole issue of Scotland's role at Westminster remains dynamic and what is stated in this chapter may only be correct at the time of writing. As the reality of devolved government in the United Kingdom settles into a more established pattern, there will an inevitable reconsideration of the way in which Westminster deals with Scottish business.

This chapter will describe briefly the key publications of the Westminster Parliament and concentrate on the electronic sources made freely available as these greatly facilitate any search for Parliamentary information. This is particularly significant because these sources enable a user to access Parliamentary material without recourse to a major reference library. It must be remembered also that these publications are the essential source for material on Scotland prior to the devolution settlement.

UK Parliament

Parliamentary Debates (Hansard)

Parliamentary Debates, popularly known as Hansard, is a substantially verbatim record of every word spoken in both Houses of Parliament and is published in a variety of frequencies - daily, weekly, and bound volumes for both Houses. The most important aspects of Hansard are its arrangement by column rather than page and that there are two separate sequences for debates and oral questions, and written answers. The major portion of each day's Hansard records speeches made in debates on legislation or matters of the day.

House of Commons Official Report: Parliamentary Debates (Hansard)
(http://www.publications.parliament.uk/pa/cm/cmhansrd.htm)

Frequently, each day's business begins with oral questions to Ministers. Written questions and their answers appear at the end of the record of the day's debates. As with the **Official Report** of the Scottish Parliament, the answers to these questions can be a source of valuable policy and statistical information not otherwise available. The printed daily issues of Hansard are not indexed and the weekly issues carry an index to oral and written answers only, arranged alphabetically by government department. Bound volumes contain an index derived from the House of Commons Library's Parliamentary On-Line Indexing Service (POLIS) (see below). The indexes cover both debates and questions and include entries for individual MPs. In addition, sessional indexes are published covering the whole of a Parliamentary session.

Westminster Hall

Since November 1999, the House has had parallel sittings in an additional chamber known as Westminster Hall. Debates in Westminster Hall are on constituency matters and other issues which the House would normally be unable to debate.

The **House of Commons Hansard** (http://www.parliament.the-stationery-office.co.uk/pa/cm/cmhansrd.htm) homepage contains the five most recent editions of Hansard, in full-text, arranged in reverse date order. There are entries for each of the relevant sections of the printed Hansard - Oral questions and debates, Westminster Hall and Written Answers. Clicking on the relevant entry will bring up a list of contents for that day, from which the full text can be retrieved. The new edition of Commons Hansard is made available each day at 9.00 a.m.

Previous editions of Commons Hansard for the current Parliamentary session are listed below the daily, arranged monthly, in reverse date order. Click on the relevant month to bring up a listing of all issues of the daily Hansard for that month.

At the bottom of the page are links to the 'bound volumes' of Commons Hansard available electronically. Click on the relevant Parliamentary session and this will bring up a listing of the bound volumes for that session, arranged in reverse volume and chronological order. An index to each volume is also available by clicking on the link to access.

If users are unsure of the date required or want to search Commons Hansard for a particular topic, it is advisable to use the **Search** (http://www.parliament.the-stationery-office.co.uk/cgi-bin/empower?DB=ukparl) option on the Parliament web-site. It is important to note, however, that the UK Parliament web-site has one **search engine** covering the whole site, so it is important that users learn how to use the search engine efficiently. It is always advisable to read the **help documentation** (http://www.parliament.the-stationery-office.co.uk/empower/livery/tso/em_help.htm), which is also available on the web-site.

To search the Commons Hansard specifically, ensure that the Commons Hansard option is chosen in the document type box. Users can restrict searches further by selecting how many search terms need to be present in the document. By default, the search will look for documents that match **any** query terms. To search for documents that mus*t* contain all of the search terms, use the matching **all** query terms option from the drop-down list. There is also a match 50% of query terms option available. Where possible, limit the search by date also.

For more guidance on how to use the UK Parliament search engine, see below under UK Parliament web-site.

House of Lords Hansard
(http://www.parliament.the-stationery-office.co.uk/pa/ld/ldhansrd.htm)

The **House of Lords Hansard** (http://www.parliament.the-stationery-office.co.uk/pa/ld/ldhansrd.htm) homepage contains links to three separate pages containing different versions of the Lords Hansard.

- **House of Lords Daily Debates** (http://www.parliament.the-stationery-office.co.uk/pa/ld199900/ldhansrd/pdvn/home.htm). This database contains the full and uncorrected text of the most recent versions of the Lords Hansard. When in session, the text for the current sitting day is made available at 9.00 a.m. the following morning.
- **House of Lords Bound Volume Debates** (http://www.parliament.the-stationery-office.co.uk/pa/ld/ldse9900.htm). A list of the volume editions of Hansard that are available for browsing on the Internet. They are arranged in reverse date order. Clicking on the relevant entry will produce a list of the contents for that volume, from which the full text can be retrieved.
- **House of Lords Bound Volume Indexes** (http://www.parliament.the-stationery-office.co.uk/pa/ld/ldbvindx.htm). The full text of the Volume Indexes to the House of Lords Parliamentary Debates (Hansard). A full explanation is available, including terms of references and abbreviations in the **introduction** (http://www.parliament.the-stationery-office.co.uk/pa/ld/ldbvintr.htm) page.

If users are unsure of the date required or want to search Lords Hansard for a particular topic, it is advisable to use the **Search** (http://www.parliament.the-stationery-office.co.uk/cgi-bin/empower?DB=ukparl) option on the Parliament web-site. It is important to note, however, that the UK Parliament web-site has one **search engine** covering the whole site, so it is important that users learn how to use the search engine efficiently. It is always advisable to read the **help documentation** (http://www.parliament.the-stationery-office.co.uk/empower/livery/tso/em_help.htm) which is also available on the web-site.

To search the Lords Hansard specifically, ensure that the Lords Hansard option is chosen in the document type box. Users can restrict search further by selecting how many search terms need to be present in the document. By default, the search will look for documents that match **any** query terms. To search for documents that must contain all of the search terms, use the matching **all** query terms option from the drop-down list. There is also a match 50% of query terms option available. Where possible, limit the search by date also.

For more guidance on how to use the UK Parliament search engine see below under UK Parliament web-site.

Key Parliamentary Publications

There are five main classes of Parliamentary Papers – House of Commons Bills, House of Commons Papers, Command Papers, House of Lords Bills and House of Lords Papers. For the purposes of this guide, only the Command Papers and House of Commons Papers series will be discussed.

House of Commons papers

This series includes some very important Parliamentary publications which cannot be ignored, particularly in a Scottish context. The House of Commons Papers series includes papers produced to support the deliberations of the House and its Committees, as well as final reports. While there are a number of categories of papers included, the most valuable types of document encompassed in this series are the papers of Select Committees (including reports, evidence and minutes of proceedings), the minutes of proceedings of Standing Committees and the Annual Reports and Accounts of certain public bodies which are required to be laid before the House.

Select Committees examine the work of particular government departments and investigate issues within their departmental remits. Evidence (both oral and written) presented to any Committee is published in the House of Commons Paper series with a lower case suffix to identify the particular serial part (e.g. the second day's evidence might be HC 11-ii of 1997-98). Each topic has a distinct number but evidence for topics investigated over more than one Session will be given a new Paper number for the new Session. Most evidence is eventually reprinted in the Committee's Report and, frequently, Reports run to more than one volume. In such cases, the individual volumes are identified by upper case suffixes (e.g. HC 11-I, HC 11-II). Each Session, Select Committees also print Minutes of their proceedings as a record of their work.

All Standing Committees' Minutes of Proceedings also appear as House of Commons Papers but the debates of the individual Committees are probably more useful documents. Many public and other autonomous bodies present their Annual Reports and Accounts to Parliament and these appear as part of the House of Commons Papers series. Increasingly, such documents relating to Scotland also appear as Scottish Executive Papers (e.g. Erskine Bridge accounts 1999-2000 appear as HC 223 2000-2001 and SE/2001/67).

Papers are giving a unique running number beginning afresh each Session and it important to refer to a particular Paper by number and Session (e.g. HC 406 1998-99). Numerical lists of all Papers appear in each year's *Stationery Office Catalogue*. With the various changes in publishing papers over the last thirty years, documents from some bodies have never been included and some have disappeared making it difficult to trace and get access to them.

Many House of Commons papers are now available on the parliament web-site (http://www.parliament.uk) by selecting **House of Commons** (http://www.parliament.the-stationery-office.co.uk/pa/cm/cmhome.htm) and, then, **House of Commons Publications on the Internet** (http://www.parliament.the-stationery-office.co.uk/pa/cm/cmpubns.htm). At present, all Select Committee reports from the start of the 1997-98 Session are available but users have to work back year by year. Since 1998, minutes of evidence on new investigations are available while the beginning of Session 1999-200 saw the addition of uncorrected transcripts of ministerial evidence on the day following submission.

There are also a small number of **House of Commons papers** (http://www.official-documents.co.uk/menu/commons.htm) available on the **Official Documents** section (http://www.official-documents.co.uk) of the **TSO** web-site (http://www.the-stationery-office.co.uk/).

It is possible to **search** (http://www.official-documents.co.uk/cgi-bin/empower?DB=off-doc) the Official Documents section of the TSO website. The Boolean operators AND, NOT, OR can be used by clicking the Boolean option. For more information on the Official Documents web-site see below.

Command papers

Command Papers are government papers laid before Parliament to convey information or decisions considered by the Government to be necessary to be drawn to the attention of either or both Houses. Once again, the series has a variety of types of paper. These include state papers (e.g. treaties), government proposals for legislation and policy documents (often referred to as White Papers), reports of Royal Commissions and other major Committees of Inquiry, departmental reports and the Annual Reports or statistics from certain public bodies (e.g. Criminal Statistics England and Wales).

Command Papers are numbered within a particular series and it is very important to use the correct prefix when looking for, or referring to them. These series are:
C 1 to C 9550: 1870-1899
Cd 1 to Cd 9239: 1900-1918
Cmd 1 to Cmd 9889: 1919-1956
Cmnd 1 to Cmnd 9927: 1956 to 7 November 1986
Cm 1 - : 2 November 1986 to date.

Once again, the TSO *Daily List* and *The Stationery Office Catalogue* are valuable finding tools and all parliamentary papers are indexed in POLIS (see below).

Many **Command papers** (http://www.official-documents.co.uk/menu/compap.htm) are now available on the **Official Documents** section (http://www.official-documents.co.uk) of the **TSO** web-site (http://www.the-stationery-office.co.uk/). The papers are arranged alphabetically by title.

It is also possible to **search** (http://www.official-documents.co.uk/cgi-bin/empower?DB=off-doc), the Official Documents section of the TSO web-site. The Boolean operators AND, NOT, OR can be used by clicking the Boolean option. For more information on the Official Documents web-site (see below).

It is also important to note that many Command papers are available electronically on the web-site of the responsible government department or ministry.

Weekly Information Bulletin

The *Weekly Information Bulletin*, produced by the House of Commons Information Office, is the authoritative guide to the current and forthcoming business of the House of Commons, plus some details for the House of Lords. It is produced weekly when the House is in Session and includes the following information each week:

▶ Business of the House of Commons for the preceding week,

▶ Forthcoming business of the House of Commons and the House of Lords (i.e. for the current week),

▶ Complete, cumulative list of Public Bills before Parliament for the session,

▶ Select and Standing Committees, membership, publications, public meetings, and forthcoming reports/enquiries announced,

▶ European Communities Documents received in the past week,

▶ White Papers and Green Papers received during the week,

▶ State of the Parties in the House of Commons.

The **Weekly Information Bulletin** (http://www.parliament.the-stationery-office.co.uk/pa/cm/cmwib.htm) from October 1996 onwards, arranged in reverse date order, is available in full text on the UK Parliament web-site.

Sessional Information Digest

This is a digest of information, produced by the House of Commons Information Office, and is a cumulation of the *Weekly Information Bulletin*, without the full bibliographical details. It includes lists and indexes of Select Committees and their reports, legislation, White and Green Papers, together with much on the work and documents of the House of Commons.

> The **Sessional Information Digest** (http://www.parliament.the-stationery-office. co.uk/pa/cm/cmsid.htm) for Sessions 1995-96 onwards, arranged in reverse date order, is available in full text on the UK Parliament web-site.

UK Parliament web-site

(http://www.parliament.uk/hophome.htm)

UK Parliament is the United Kingdom Parliament's web service. It contains a vast array of information and documentation about the Parliament generally and its two Houses. Information on how to access the important documentation of the Westminster Parliament via the web has already been covered in detail above. In this section, general information about the web-site, navigation and searching will be discussed. In addition, an introduction to the Parliamentary databases, which have been made available free on the UK Parliament web-site, will be provided.

The **Parliamentary Internet site-map** (http://www.parliament.uk/parliament/ sitemap.htm) and **Index** page (http://www.parliament.uk/parliament/index.htm) both provide useful overviews for users unsure about what information is contained on the web-site. The **House of Commons** (http://www.parliament.uk/commons/HSECOM.HTM) and the **House of Lords** (http://www.publications.parliament.uk/pa/ld/ldhome.htm) each have separate home pages which provide links to important information and documentation on the respective House. Alternatively, users can choose to search the whole of the Parliament web-site using the Parliament's **search engine** (http://www.parliament. the-stationery-office.co.uk/cgi-bin/empower?DB=ukparl) (see below for detailed guidance).

Searching the UK Parliament Pages
(http://www.parliament.the-stationery-office.co.uk/cgi-bin/empower?DB=ukparl)

The UK Parliament web-site **search engine** has very useful **help documentation** (http://www.parliament.the-stationery-office.co.uk/empower/livery/tso/em_help.htm) which users should read in order to use the search engine more efficiently and effectively.

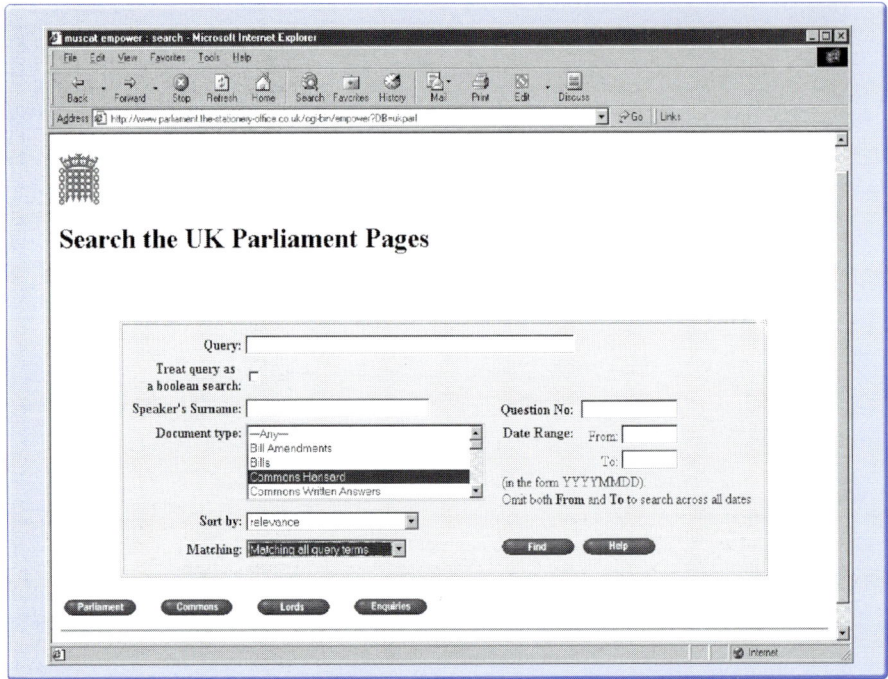

The search engine template (see above) provides a range of methods for searching the publications on the Parliamentary web-site. The Query box allows users to make a search using natural language, or by phrase (must be enclosed in double quotes e.g. ""). By clicking the Boolean checkbox under the Query box, users can turn the search terms into a Boolean Search. This enables the use of the logical operators, AND, OR and NOT between the terms to improve the search. By default, AND is assumed between all search terms. Users can also search by Speaker Name and by Question Number assigned to Parliamentary Questions by both Houses. Once the choice of method has been selected, searches can be further refined by specifying Document type (e.g. Bills or Commons Hansard) and date range.

POLIS (Parliamentary Online Indexing Service) Database
(http://www.polis.parliament.uk/)

POLIS provides an index to the proceedings and publications of both Houses of Parliament and includes the full text of Early Day Motions since May 1997. POLIS also contains many records to books and papers held by the House of Commons Library.

The database can be searched using a simple form, and the service offers easy navigation tools. To begin searching, click on the Search POLIS icon on the homepage.

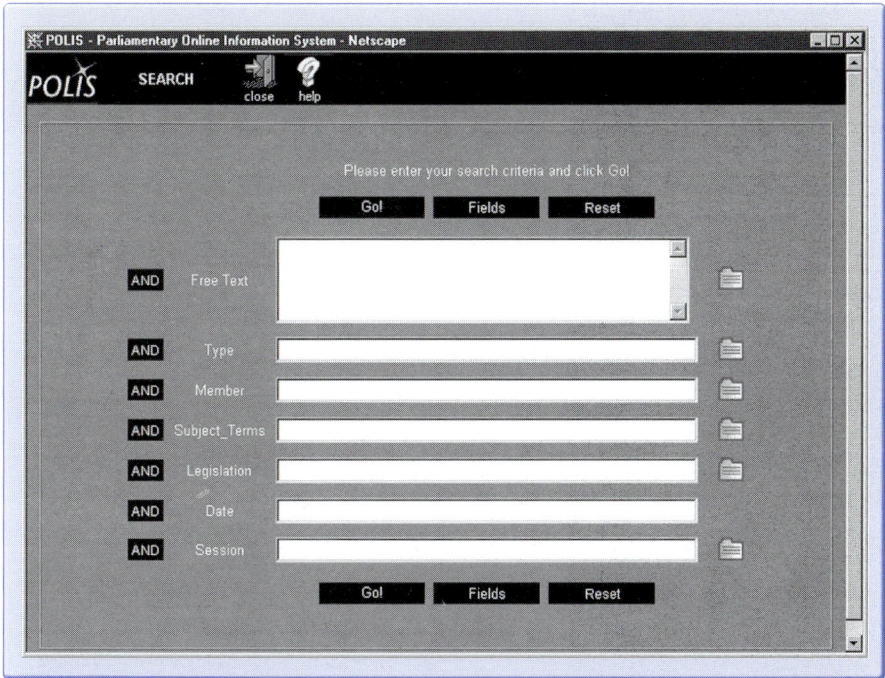

There is one text box for each of the commonly used fields in POLIS - Document type, Member, Subject, Legislation, Date and Session. Users can change the assortment of fields available by clicking the 'Fields' button and selecting and de-selecting from the list (users can restore the default fields by clicking the 'Reset' button). There is also a box for free text searching - terms that are typed here will be searched for in all fields. Boolean operators can also be used by clicking the appropriate 'AND' button. When all of the search terms are entered, click the Go! button near the top or bottom of the window. Results are presented in summary version and reverse chronological order. To see the full or document entry, click on the hypertext line (underlined title). For more detailed information on searching POLIS and downloading results, click on the Help icon at the top of the search screen.

The site also has links to a **Guide to Parliament** (http://www.parliament.uk/parliament/ guide/parliamt.htm), the House of Commons Information Office **Factsheets** (http://www.parliament.uk/commons/lib/fact.htm), discussing the working, history and membership of Parliament, and a **List of Members and committees** (http://www.parliament.uk/commons/lib/lists.htm), in addition to other portals for schools and general users.

Early Day Motions Database
(http://edm.ais.co.uk/)

Early Day Motion (EDM) is the term used to describe notices of motions given by Members that are not generally expected to be debated. Effectively, the tabling of an EDM is a device to draw attention to an issue, and to elicit support for it by means of inviting other Members to add their signatures to the motion. Members may also table amendments to existing motions. The database is updated overnight with the titles of new EDMs added the previous day, and signatures added to existing motions. The full text of new EDMs is added two days after they have been tabled.

The toolbar along the top of the page allows users a number of ways to access EDM information.

- ▶ **Search** - see below for more detail.
- ▶ **EDM** - this returns a list showing the titles of EDMs and amendments tabled so far this session, in groups of 50, with their reference number, the name of the primary sponsor and the number of signatures added to date.
- ▶ **Members** - this returns a list showing the names of Members of Parliament, in alphabetical order, with their constituency, political party and the number of EDMs signed in the current parliamentary session.
- ▶ **Session** - the database defaults to the current Parliamentary session but the information for previous sessions by using this drop-down box.

Users can **search** (http://edm.ais.co.uk/weblink/html/search.html) the EDM database by EDM number, by Text or Subject Heading, or by Members name. To use the Text or Subject Heading option, type the search criteria in the 'search for' box and click search button. Please note that 'quotation marks' are required to search for a phrase, and use + to search for more than one word. Searches can be refined by using the 'Extend search to' button. To use the Member search box, names should be cited using the format surname/first name or initial.

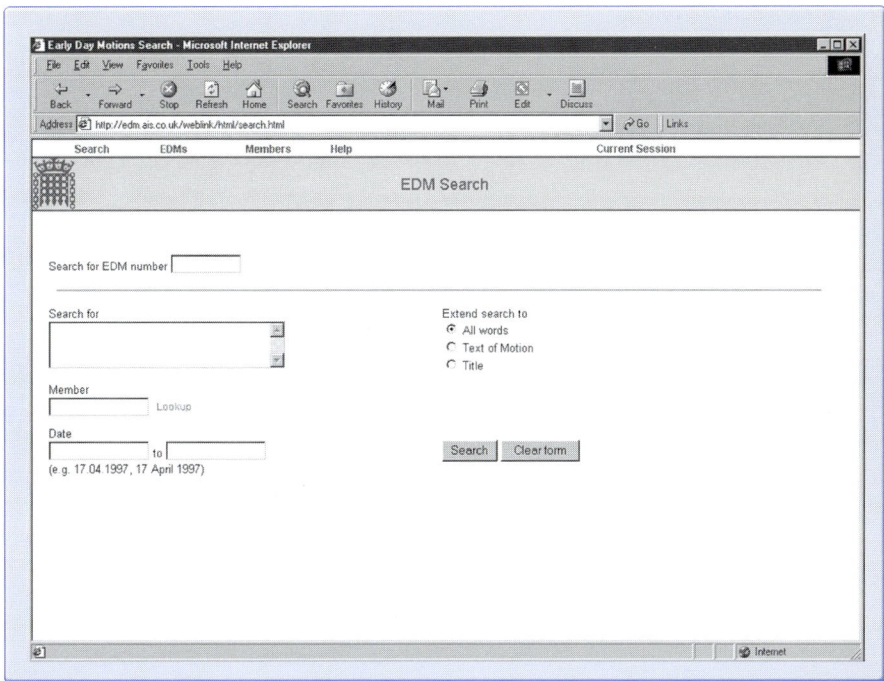

Other Useful Information on the UK Parliament

House of Commons Information Office
(http://www.parliament.uk/commons/lib/pio.htm)

The House of Commons Information Office was established in 1978, under the name Public Information Office, as part of the House of Commons Library to act as a central answering point for enquiries from the public which relate to the work, publications, proceedings and history of the House of Commons. As well as providing the *Weekly Information Bulletin* and the *Sessional Information Digest,* it also provides the following documentation and information which users might find useful:

▶ **Factsheets** (http://www.parliament.uk/commons/lib/fact.htm) - brief informative descriptions of various facets of the House of Commons.

▶ **List of Members of Parliament** (http://www.parliament.uk/commons/lib/MEM.HTM) - lists arranged alphabetically and by constituency and county. Also provides up to date current membership lists of the members of Cabinet and all of the Select Committees.

House of Commons Library

Library Research Papers (http://www.parliament.uk/commons/lib/research/ rpintro.htm) - full text (in pdf format) of Research Papers compiled for the benefit of Members of Parliament by the staff of the House of Commons Library. They are an occasional series, numbered by year and sequence of publication, and usually deal with topics of current Parliamentary interest. They aim to be politically impartial and contain factual information as well as a range of opinions on each subject covered.

TSO Official Documents web-site
(http://www.official-documents.co.uk/)

This web-site, developed by The Stationery Office, provides access to some, but by no means all, official documents published by The Stationery Office and other authoritative bodies. Users can access the information in a number of ways - by **date** (http://www.official-documents.co.uk/menu/bydate.htm), **alphabetical by title** (http://www.official-documents.co.uk/menu/bytitle.htm), by **government department** (http://www.official-documents.co.uk/menu/bydept.htm); or arranged by **document type** (http://www.official-documents.co.uk/menu/uk.htm) (e.g. Command Papers, House of Commons Papers).

It is also possible to **search** (http://www.official-documents.co.uk/cgi-bin/empower?DB=off-doc), the **Official Documents** section of the TSO web-site. The Boolean operators AND, NOT, OR can be used by clicking the Boolean option. The **search** site does have a set of help pages accessed by clicking on the help icon at the top of the screen. However, this provides generic information about using that search engine generally, and does not assist searching on the **Official Documents** section specifically.

UK Online
(http://www.ukonline.gov.uk/online/ukonline/home)

The aim of ukonline is to provide comprehensive access to government information published on the Internet. The basic structure is the same for each section. Following a brief introduction, users have the option to choose items from a list or submit a search query. Whichever method is used, the portal attempts to target and return only the information requested. This is important given the vast amount of government information available. It consists of three major sections:

▶ **Life Episodes** (http://www.ukonline.gov.uk/online/ukonline/leHome) - provides legal information on common events in life (e.g. having a baby, moving home, dealing with bereavement). Select an episode from those listed for more information and links to government resources.

▶ **CitizenSpace** (http://www.ukonline.gov.uk/online/citizenspace/) - designed to allow citizens to become more involved in the democratic process. The site contains information on current government consultations; provides information on MPs, elections and policy-making.

▶ **Quick Find Section** (http://www.ukonline.gov.uk/online/ukonline/quickFind) - for speedy access to any government information. This section allows users to search by keyword using a purple search box or by a particular area (see below).

▶ **Search** - to use the quick find search option, enter keywords or a complete sentence or phrase in the search box provided and click the 'search' button on the right. Users be more specific by changing the default buttons underneath the search box. Boolean searching is also possible allowing users to create specific relationships between words by using brackets and the operators OR, NOT, AND, and NEAR. There is also an **Advanced Search** option (http://www.ukonline.gov.uk/online/ukonline/adQuickFind) and a **Help** facility (http://www.ukonline.gov.uk/online/ukonline/helpQuickFind).

▶ **Quick Find** also includes information about and links to:

▶ **Central Government Services** (http://www.ukonline.gov.uk/online/ukonline/centralServices) - links to the web-sites of government departments and agencies.

▶ **Local Government Services** (http://www.ukonline.gov.uk/online/ukonline/localGovernment) – links to local government web-sites.

▶ **Local Services** (http://www.ukonline.gov.uk/online/ukonline/localServices) - local information about national services (e.g. health, education, social security).

▶ **Forms and Legal Documents** - which directs users to the **Direct Access Government** web-site (http://porch.ccta.gov.uk/dag/dag2000.nsf).

▶ **Government News Releases** - which directs users to the **Central Office of Information** web-site (http://www.nds.coi.gov.uk/coi/coipress.nsf).

▶ **Government Publications** - which directs users to the **UK Official Documents** page (http://www.official-documents.co.uk/menu/uk.htm) on the TSO web-site.

Presently, ukonline also provides a couple of other very useful sections:

▶ **Newsroom** (http://www.ukonline.gov.uk/online/ukonline/newsCentre) - which provides regularly updated links to the main news and events from government and devolved administrations in Northern Ireland, Scotland and Wales. The 'Political parties' section provides links to the web-sites of political parties in the UK & Scottish Parliaments, European Parliament, and the devolved Assemblies in Northern Ireland and Wales. The 'Webcasts and transcripts' provides links to broadcasts by the Prime Minister, recent sessions of Prime Minister's Questions from the House of Commons, statements by the Prime Minister and broadcasts of other special events.

▶ [Site Map](http://www.ukonline.gov.uk/online/ukonline/UKOLSM) (http://www.ukonline.gov.uk/online/ukonline/UKOLSM), which provides users with a navigation tool for the whole ukonline site.

Scottish Matters at Westminster

The UK Parliament retains the right to debate Scottish matters and this is generally done by the Departmental Select Committee or the Scottish Grand Committee.

Scottish Affairs Departmental Select Committee

This Committee can examine the work, policy and expenditure of the Scotland Office and the Advocate General for Scotland and has the power to take evidence in Scotland. Committee reports and the evidence from its various sessions are published as House of Commons Papers by The Stationery Office in the same way as other Select Committee reports. Recently, the Scottish Affairs Committee has investigated and reported on Poverty in Scotland (HC 59, 1999-2000) and has been considering the work of BBC Scotland and the Broadcasting Council for Scotland (HC 176, 1999-2000), the work of the Scotland Office since devolution (HC 390, 1999-2000) and the drinks industry in Scotland, (HC 973, 1999-2000). Like all other Select Committee reports, Minutes of Evidence for each sitting are printed as prepared (e.g. HC 59-i are the Minutes of 3 November 1999) and these are engrossed with the proceedings of the Committee and appendices when the final report is published.

The reports of other departmental Select Committees can also have a relevance to Scotland (e.g. the 24th Report of the Committee of Public Accounts investigated the Passport Delays of Summer 1999, HC 208, 1999-2000).

The publications of the **Scottish Affairs Select Committee** (http://www.parliament. the-stationery-office.co.uk/pa/cm/cmscotaf.htm) from Session 1997-98 onwards are available in full text on the UK Parliament web-site. The publications of the current Parliamentary session appear, in reverse chronological order on the home page with links to previous sessions at the bottom of each page. There are separate pages for each session.

Minutes of evidence from recent meetings appear at the top of the page and published reports (which also include the proceedings) appear further down. The date of publication, House of Commons Paper Number and ISBN are also listed.

Scottish Grand Committee

The Scottish Grand Committee is a standing committee of the House of Commons, whose membership is the 72 MPs for Scottish constituencies. Since 1994, its powers and functions have changed and it now regularly meets in Scotland as well as at Westminster. It can transact a range of parliamentary business relevant to Scotland and is considered a useful mechanism for Scottish MPs to highlight UK-wide policies having an impact on Scotland. In addition, it considers the principles of all Public Bills considered by the Speaker to relate exclusively to Scotland.

In 2000, the Scottish Grand Committee met on four occasions and debated the New Deal and Youth Employment, the effect of the high pound, the size of the Scottish Parliament and employment policy, while in 2001 the Committee debated the oil and gas industry. Matters for debate can be chosen on two days by the leader of the largest opposition party in Scotland and another two days' debate are at the disposal of the next largest opposition party. The meetings of the Grand Committee are not exclusively Scottish. Debates can be led by Secretaries and Ministers of State (e.g. the Secretary of State for Trade and Industry opened the debate on employment policy in July 2000). When the Grand Committee meets, statements can be made on government policy and action. For example, a statement on action to combat drug abuse was made by a Minister of State at the Cabinet Office prior to the debate on the Scottish oil and gas industry. Short adjournment debates may be raised by members of the Committee and tend to follow the main debate (e.g. civil service jobs in Dundee). At present, there does not appear to be a web version of the proceedings of meetings of the Scottish Grand Committee.

Scottish Questions

One significant change since devolution has been the reduction in the time allowed for oral questions to the Secretary of State for Scotland or the Advocate General, which still takes place approximately every four weeks. Since the establishment of the Scottish Parliament and Executive, the time allocated for the Scotland Office has been reduced from an hour to thirty minutes. Questions can be asked by any Member from a UK constituency but they must relate to the Secretary of State's own responsibilities and not to devolved matters.

A House of Commons Delegated Legislation Standing Committee (DLSC) will still consider matters such as regulations and amendments covering the representation of the people and elections.

When searching the Parliament web-site for Scottish Questions, the most effective method is through the UK Parliament **search engine** (http://www.parliament.the-stationery-office.co.uk/cgi-bin/empower?DB=ukparl). Searching for questions on specific issues can produce very variable results and seems to rely on the indexing of terms. In many respects, it may be easier for users to browse through the questions asked on the occasions when Scottish ministers appear (on a monthly basis). Users should remember that such questions are entered in Hansard as Oral Answers to Questions: Scotland and, therefore, the most effective method of searching is to use the following search string in the 'Query' box - Oral and Questions and Scotland, remembering to click the option for Boolean searching. Highlight 'Commons Hansard' in the Document type box, and the 'Sort By' option should be set to Date and then Relevance and the 'Matching' option to Matching all Query Items. This will return results in reverse chronological order.

Scottish Private Bills

One other area of Westminster involvement is where Scottish Private Bills deal with 'reserved' matters and these continue to proceed by way of a 'draft Provisional Order' subject to confirmation by a Bill introduced in the Westminster Parliament. Recent private legislation relating to Scotland includes the Comhairle Nan Eilean Siar (Eriskay Causeway) Order Confirmation Act 2000 c.i, allowing the construction of a causeway between South Uist and Eriskay and the Railtrack (Waverley Station) Order Confirmation Act 2000 c.vi, to improve and develop the station. Currently, such private legislation as the Balloch Footbridge, City of Edinburgh Rapid Transit and Strathclyde Tram Orders have been allowed to proceed.

Scottish Standing Committees

There are two Scottish Standing Committees which debate Bills certified as relating exclusively to Scotland by the Speaker. It is usual for the First Scottish Standing Committee to consider the Committee stage of Government Bills, while the Second Scottish Standing Committee looks at the Committee stage of Private Members' Bills. At the time of writing, the Scottish Standing Committees appear to be inactive, having last met in February and May 1999 respectively. Certainly, there does not appear to be a web version of the proceedings of meetings of the Scottish Standing Committees and their work and functions may be subject to review. At present, it is the intention of the government that the UK Parliament will not normally legislate on any devolved matter except with the agreement of the devolved legislature.

Scotland Office

The creation of the Scottish Executive and the transfer of 'devolved' matters considerably altered the size and responsibilities of the former Scottish Office. The Scotland Office is the government department charged with ensuring that Scottish interests are represented within the United Kingdom Government. At present, it is split into three administrative divisions covering constitutional and parliamentary, economy and industry, and home and social matters. In addition, the department includes the Office of the Solicitor to the Advocate General, Ministerial Private Offices, including the Legal Secretariat to the Advocate General, a Finance and Administration branch and an Information branch.

With the creation of the Scottish Parliament, the Lord Advocate and the Solicitor General for Scotland transferred to the Scottish Executive. A new office, that of Advocate General for Scotland, was created to give opinions and provide informal advice to the UK Government, particularly in relation to Scots law. The Advocate General also gives advice on more general issues of common interest to the UK such as European law and Human Rights. Under the terms of the Scotland Act, the Advocate General has a statutory role in relation to devolution. Decisions on the competence of Bills of the Scottish Parliament can be referred to the Judicial Committee of the Privy Council. The Advocate General can also raise other proceedings on devolution issues in the Scottish Courts and Privy Council. The Scotland Office web-site has a page providing a description of the office of **Advocate General** and contact information (http://www. scottishsecretary.gov.uk/ags.htm). The site also has a page of **contact information** for the Scotland Office (http://www.scottishsecretary.gov.uk/contact.htm) and **links** to other useful sites (http://www.scottishsecretary.gov.uk/links.htm).

Matters in which the Scotland Office has been involved include the development of UK policy in relation to 'reserved' matters notably in relation to those affecting Scotland's economy. It continues to be responsible for such issues as the designation of assisted areas, the promotion of overseas trade interests, government decisions affecting the oil and gas industry in Scotland and defence industries, regulation of the energy and financial services sectors in Scotland, and cross-border air and sea transportation. Other relevant subjects have been the review of the operation of the Post Office network, the preparation of the Communications White Paper, the review of Gaelic broadcasting; and the operation of the New Deal.

The Scotland Office contributes to inquiries by the Scottish Affairs Select Committee (e.g. replying to reports on Tourism in Scotland (April 2000)). Similarly, it contributes to debates in the Scottish Grand Committee and has submitted written evidence to an inquiry by the Scottish Parliament's European Committee into the operation of European Structural Funds in Scotland. It has a major role in supporting Ministers in the presentation of UK policies in Scotland (e.g. the promotion of the Minimum Income Guarantee, the Children's Tax Credit, the National Minimum Wage and Equal Pay for women). The Scotland Office also funds the Private Legislation Procedure Office for Scotland and the Parliamentary Boundary Commission for Scotland.

Its **web-site** (http://www.scottishsecretary.gov.uk/index.htm) is the principal source for information on the department's activities. In addition to **news releases** on a wide range of issues (http://www.scottishsecretary.gov.uk/press.htm), the site has a **publications page** (http://www.scottishsecretary.gov.uk/pub.htm) which includes links to the departmental report and the Boundary Commission annual report. There are also links to biographical information about the **Scottish Ministers** (http://www.scottishsecretary. gov.uk/ministers.htm), the texts of **speeches** made by Scottish Ministers (http://www. scottishsecretary.gov.uk/speeches.htm) and a description of the **role** of the department, under **What We Do** (http://www.scottishsecretary.gov.uk/what.htm) which includes a detailed list of '**reserved**' matters.

Other Government Departments

It would be impractical in a guide of this nature to detail the workings and organisation of every UK government agency and department. On the other hand, it is essential for users to be aware of sources that will assist in locating information and publications from them, particularly when they relate to 'reserved' matters or have a UK-wide relevance. The whole network of departmental publishing has resulted in a confusing pattern of material produced, ranging from detailed surveys and reports to information leaflets and circulars.

Some impression of the complexity and scale of this aspect of official publishing can be formed from a consideration of the printed *Catalogue of British Official Publications Not Published by The Stationery Office*, produced by Chadwyck-Healey. This lists publications from over 500 organisations financed or controlled in some way by the British Government, including government departments, but not published by The Stationery Office. The Catalogue commenced in 1980 and is produced six times a year with an annual cumulative volume, which now includes over 15,000 items. Each issue is arranged alphabetically by publishing body and carries full bibliographical information, an index of source addresses and an alphabetical index of names and subjects. This publication is the most comprehensive source for governmental publishing but does not cover circulars and material of an ephemeral nature. It also excludes specialised material, such as Ordnance Survey maps, already well catalogued.

This catalogue is also available commercially through the Internet as **UKOP Online** (http://www.ukop.co.uk/info/index.html), an authoritative guide to over 450,000 government publications in the United Kingdom, covering the period from 1980. There are hypertext links from records to an increasing number of full text documents from the beginning of 1997. UKOP Online combines the official catalogue of The Stationery Office publications with the *Catalogue of Official Publications not Published by The Stationery Office.*

Users can also access individual government bodies and agencies through HM Government's **UK online web-site** (http://www.ukonline.gov.uk) (see above).

Scotland and the European Union

T he principal aims of this chapter are twofold. Firstly, it introduces users to Scottish Official Publications and information sources on or about the European Union and its policies. Secondly, it offers a general introduction to the main sources of official information, both printed and electronic, available from the European Union and its institutions.

The inclusion of a chapter on the European Union is important because its laws and policies impact on all aspects of Scottish life, particularly through the provision of regional development aid, measures to reduce unemployment, support for training for rural activities and small businesses, research and development funding, educational exchange programmes, and through the protection of the environment. While relations with the European Union are a 'reserved' matter and the responsibility of the UK Government, the Scottish Executive and Scottish Parliament are responsible for the implementation and implications of all European obligations for which they have devolved responsibility.

The **Memorandum of Understanding and Supplementary Agreements** (http://www. scotland.gov.uk/library2/memorandum/) document sets out the principles that underlie relations between the UK Government and the devolved administrations and **Section B1: Concordat on Co-ordination of European Union Policy Issues - Scotland** (http://www.scotland.gov.uk/library2/memorandum/mous-04.htm) specifically deals with the handling of matters with an EU dimension. There are also a number of European policy issues where distinctive Scottish interests are apparent. These include fishing, agriculture, environment, structural funds, education and justice matters. For more information on these matters, see **European Union Policies and Scotland** (http://www.scotland.gov.uk/euoffice/scot_eu1.asp#1), a background note available on the **Scottish Executive EU Office** web-site (http://www.scotland.gov.uk/euoffice/).

It is also important to remember that the relationship between Scotland and the European Union is not confined to the Scottish Executive and the Scottish Parliament. Scottish representatives in European Union institutions also play an important part. The eight Scottish Members of the European Parliament (MEPs), four members of the Committee of the Regions and two members on the Economic and Social Committee all lobby and argue for Scottish interests.

The choice of publications and web-sites listed in this chapter is, inevitably, selective but is based on experience of use and reliability. Publications and information produced in Scotland are dealt with in the first half before moving on to the publications of the European Union and its institutions.

Scottish Sources of European Union Information

Scottish Parliament

The most influential body in the Scottish Parliament with regard to European matters is the **European Committee** (http://www.scottish.parliament.uk/official_report/cttee/europe.htm). The European Committee's remit is to consider and report on proposals for, and the implementation of, European Communities legislation and any other European Union issue. The Committee produces Official Reports, Agenda and Minutes of Proceedings (available only electronically) and Reports (which are issued as SP Papers) all of which are available on the Committee home page (http://www.scottish.parliament.uk/official_report/cttee/europe.htm). The European Committee also produces an electronic newsletter called *Europe Matters*, which is intended to keep interested parties informed of the Committee's activities and is available, in pdf format, on their web-site. For more detail on the publishing output of Scottish Parliament Committees, both printed and electronic, see Chapter 1.

To help understand the process whereby European legislation is implemented into Scots law, the passage of **The Sulphur Content of Liquid Fuels (Scotland) Regulations 2000** is given as an example (Fig. 4) *(over)*.

Fig. 4 From EU to Scottish Legislation - Implementation in Scotland of EC

1997*	1998*	1999	Oct 1999
European Commission	European Commission	European Council Directive	Scottish Executive Consultation Paper
Proposal for a Council Directive relating to a reduction of the sulphur content of certain liquid fuels and amending Directive 93/12/EEC	Amended proposal for a Council Directive relating to a reduction of the sulphur content of certain liquid fuels and amending Directive 93/12/EEC	Council Directive 1999/32/EC of 26 April 1999 relating to a reduction in the sulphur content of certain liquid fuels and amending Directive 93/12/EEC	Implementation in Scotland of EC Directive 1999/32/EC on the Sulphur Content of Certain Liquid Fuels
COM/1997/88/ Final	COM/1998/385/ Final	Council Directive 1999/32/EC	

---

*   The Commission proposal went through the full European legislative process. The PRE-Lex** database entry for COM/1997/88 final and the Legislative Assembly database (OEIL)*** for Council Directive 1999/32/EC both provide full listings of all documents issued by the various institutions throughout the lengthy process.

**   PRELEX database (http://europa.eu.int/prelex/rech_simple.cfm?CL=en) - monitors the interinstitutional decision-making process. PreLex follows all Commission proposals (legislative and budgetary files, conclusions of the international agreements) and communications from their transmission to the Council or to European Parliament until their adoption or their rejection by the Council, their adoption by Parliament or their withdrawal by the Commission.

Directive 1999/32/EC on the Sulphur Content of Certain Liquid Fuels

June 2000	June 2000	June 2000	December 2000
Scottish Parliament Transport and Environment Committee	Scottish Parliament Subordinate Legislation Committee	Scottish Statutory Instrument	Scottish Executive Leaflet
The Sulphur Content of Liquid Fuels (Scotland) Regulations 2000	The Sulphur Content of Liquid Fuels (Scotland) Regulations 2000	The Sulphur Content of Liquid Fuels (Scotland) Regulations 2000	Sulphur Limits in Liquid Fuels: information for users of heavy fuel oil and gas oil
SP OR TE 28 June 2000, col 835	SP OR SL 13 June 2000, col 245	SSI 2000 No. 169	

*** **OEIL database** (http://wwwdb.europarl.eu.int/dors/oeil/en/default.htm) - covers the activities of the institutions involved in the legislative procedure and the decision-making process. This tool should make it possible to follow and monitor the Community decision-making process and to evaluate and monitor the workload of Parliament and its committees, the Commission's annual working programme and the proposals of the different Council Presidencies. The database is updated daily.

Scottish Executive

The **Europe** section (http://www.scotland.gov.uk/whatwedo.asp?topic=europe) of the **Scottish Executive** (http://www.scotland.gov.uk/default.asp) web-site is not particularly insightful or helpful. However, the **Publications** (http://www.scotland.gov.uk/whatwedo.asp?type=pub&topic=europe) section has links to all documents published by the Executive (and Scottish Office) on European matters since 1998. The **Press Releases** (http://www.scotland.gov.uk/whatwedo.asp?type=press&topic=europe) section will keep users informed of the latest developments on EU policy.

The Scottish Executive established an **EU Office** (http://www.scotland.gov.uk/euoffice/) in Brussels to assist them in dealing with their EU-related business. It works closely with the **United Kingdom Permanent Representation (UKRep)** (http://ukrep.fco.gov.uk/), which remains responsible for representing the views of the UK as a whole to the EC institutions. The EU Office is based in **Scotland House** which it shares with **Scotland Europa** (http://www.scotlandeuropa.com/), an umbrella body representing and promoting Scottish public, private and voluntary interests in Brussels. See below (Other Useful Scottish EU Sources) for more details about this organisation.

European Commission Representation in Scotland

European Commission Representation in Scotland (http://www.cec.org.uk/scotland/index.htm) is part of the of European Commission's Representations network. The Scotland Representation, based in Edinburgh, is one of three regional offices (the others being in Cardiff and Belfast) attached to the main **UK Representation** (http://www.cec.org.uk/) office in London. The main duties of the Representation in Scotland are to advise public and private organisations, the media and much of the Scottish public on the nature and impact of EU institutions and policies.

The Representation in Scotland web-site is part of the larger UK Representation web-site which is a very useful resource indeed. The **A-Z index** (http://www.cec.org.uk/azindex/index.htm) page is a valuable introduction to the site. Users can see, at a glance, the extensive amount of information contained here and it offers easy navigation around the web-site. The UK Representation Offices of the European Commission publish a wide range of booklets, guides and newsletters that are intended both to provide information and to inform public debate. A selection of these publications can be viewed on the **publications** (http://www.cec.org.uk/info/pubs/index.htm) section of the web-site. Please note that those publications available **only** in electronic form are indicated by (E). The **Representation in Scotland** (http://www.cec.org.uk/scotland/index.htm) page provides links to three key electronic publications relating specifically to Scotland:

▶ **Scotland in Europe** (http://www.cec.org.uk/info/pubs/regional/sc/contents.htm),

- ▶ **European Funding and Scotland: A guide to the funding process** (http://www.cec.org.uk/scotland/funding.pdf),
- ▶ **Directory of EU Information Providers in Scotland** (http://www.cec.org.uk/scotland/direct.pdf).

European Parliament Office in Scotland

The **European Parliament Office in Scotland** (http://www.europarl.org.uk/office/ScotlandOfficeMain.htm), established in Edinburgh in 1999, is a branch of the **UK Office of the European Parliament** (http://www.europarl.org.uk/office/TheOfficeMain.htm) based in London. The Office in Scotland aims to help increase awareness of the European Parliament and its activities in Scotland. It does so by providing information to the public, the media, government, regional agencies and the business community about the role and activities of the Parliament itself and the European Union more generally.

The European Parliament Office in Scotland web-site is part of the larger UK Office of the European Parliament web-site which provides information on the European Parliament itself and its work, specifically in the United Kingdom and, of course, in Scotland. The **site map** (http://www.europarl.org.uk/map/MapMain.htm) section of the web-site, arranged under eight general subject headings, is a good place to start to find your way around.

Other Useful Scottish EU Sources

Scotland Europa

Scotland Europa (http://www.scotlandeuropa.com/) is a subsidiary of Scottish Enterprise. It is based in Brussels (in Scotland House, which it shares with the Scottish Executive EU Office) and provides a variety of services for its members. Around sixty Scottish organisations now subscribe to the services offered by Scotland Europa which include monthly intelligence reports by sector and briefing meetings for members by key EU institution representatives. Scotland Europa also produce a series of occasional papers called the **Scotland Europa Papers** (http://www.scotlandeuropa.com/sp_index.htm). These are intended to provide a forum for interested parties in Scotland and other European countries and regions to promote ideas and perspectives on issues that are of importance to the development of Scotland and the EU.

European Information Network in Scotland

European Information Network in Scotland (http://www.europe.org.uk/info/scotland/), developed by the Scottish European Resources Network (SERN), is part of a the larger

European Information in the UK (http://www.europe.org.uk/info/) initiative. This attempts to bring together contact details of organisations and individuals in the UK and its regions that provide EU information and advice for the general public, the academic community and business. The sites also hold addresses for EU institutions and agencies that are based in the UK, MEPs, sectoral bodies with EU interests (e.g. the TUC). The site is supported by the European Commission Representation in the UK.

Other Useful EU Sources

European Information Association (EIA)

The **European Information Association (EIA)** (http://www.eia.org.uk/eiaorg/ Default.htm) is an international body of information specialists whose aim is to develop, co-ordinate and improve access to EU information. The EIA does charge its members an annual subscription although this does entitle them to printed copies of the monthly newsletter *EIA Update* and quarterly journal *European Information,* as well as discounts on publications and electronic products produced by other publishers.

The EIA does make some of the above information available free of charge to non-members on their web-site. For example, the monthly newsletter **EIA Update** (http://www.eia.org.uk/eiaorg/newsletr.htm) appears on the web one month after members have received the printed copy, and selected articles from the Association's journal **European Information** (http://www.eia.org.uk/eiaorg/journal.htm) are also available. A few of the EIA Quick Guides have also been made available (in pdf format) see the **Publications** (http://www.eia.org.uk/eiaorg/eiapubs.htm) section of the web-site for details. Users will also find the **web-sites for EU information** (http://www.eia.org. uk/eiaorg/websites.htm) page one of the most comprehensive available.

European Union Sources

In this section the most important printed and electronic publications emanating from European Union are considered. This is, by no means, a comprehensive listing but one based on the experience of the authors. Because of the complex nature of the European Union, some background information on the principal Institutions is offered first with links to their respective web-sites given. At the end of the section some of the most important and widely used web-sites and databases will be described in detail.

Institutions of the European Union

The European Union is built on an institutional system which is the only one of its kind in the world. The Member States delegate sovereignty for certain matters to independent institutions which represent the interests of the Union as a whole, its member countries and its citizens. There are five institutions involved in running the European Union:

- ▶ **European Parliament** (http://www.europarl.eu.int/home/default_en.htm) - is elected every five years by the peoples of the Member States. The Parliament has three essential functions - to share with the Council the power to legislate, to share budgetary authority with the Council (and therefore influence EU spending) and to exercise democratic supervision over the Commission and political supervision over all EU institutions.

- ▶ **Council** (http://ue.eu.int/en/summ.htm) - is the European Union's main decision-making and legislative body representing the governments of the Member States. In addition, the Council has a number of other key responsibilities which include the framing and implementing common foreign and security policy, concluding international agreements with other states and international organisations, the co-ordination of the broad economic policies of the Member States, and the co-ordination and adoption of measures in the field of police and judicial co-operation in criminal matters.

- ▶ **Commission** (http://europa.eu.int/comm/index_en.htm) - is the executive body of the European Union. It consists of thirty-six directorates-general and specialised services. They are each headed by a director-general, who is equivalent in rank to the top civil servant in a government ministry. The directors-general report to a Commissioner, each of whom has the political and operational responsibility for one or more DGs. The Commission has three main functions - to initiate legislation on the basis of what it considers best for the Union and its citizens, to act as the guardian of the EU treaties and to ensure that EU legislation is applied correctly by the Member States, and, in its capacity as the executive body, it is responsible for implementing and managing policy.

- ▶ **Court of Justice** (http://curia.eu.int/en/index.htm) - ensures that Community law is uniformly interpreted and effectively applied. For more detailed information on the Court of Justice, see Chapter 3.

- ▶ **Court of Auditors** (http://www.eca.eu.int/) - is responsible for the auditing of EU accounts and the implementation of the budget of the European Union.

Other Bodies Supporting these Institutions

- ▶ **Economic and Social Committee** (http://www.ces.eu.int/) - a consultative body which represents the various categories of economic and social activities. It has 222 members, drawn from organisations representing employers, workers, farmers, small businesses, commerce, crafts, co-operatives, mutual benefit societies, the professions, consumers, environmentalists, families, and 'social' Non-Governmental Organisations. The Committee has to be consulted on matters relating to economic and social policy; it may also issue opinions, on its own initiative, on other matters which it considers to be important.

▶ **Committee of the Regions** (http://www.cor.eu.int/home.htm) - a consultative body which represents the interests of local and regional authorities. It has 222 members and 222 alternates composed of representatives of regional and local authorities. It has to be consulted on matters concerning regional policy, the environment and education.

▶ **European Central Bank** (http://www.ecb.int/) - is responsible for monetary policy in the Euro-area.

▶ **European Investment Bank** (http://eib.eu.int/) - is the financial institution of the European Union. It finances investment projects which contribute to the balanced development of the Union.

▶ **European Ombudsman** (http://www.euro-ombudsman.eu.int/) - deals with complaints from citizens concerning maladministration at European level

---

European Union Documents and Legislative Texts

In this section the most significant publications of the European Union institutions are described.

Official Journal of the European Communities

The *Official Journal of the European Communities (OJ)* is the principal official source of European documentation. It is published daily in 11 languages and consists of two related series - the L series (Legislation) and the C series (Information, notices and preparatory EU legislation), along with a Supplement (the S series for public tenders).

▶ **OJ L (Legislation) series** - contains EU legislation, including regulations, directives, decisions, recommendations and opinions.

▶ **OJ C (EU information and notices) series** contains summaries of judgements of the Court of Justice and the Court of First Instance, minutes of parliamentary meetings, reports of the Court of Auditors, parliamentary written questions and answers from the Council or Commission, statements from the Committee of the Regions and the Economic and Social Committee, competition notices for recruitment to the EU's institutions, calls for interest in EU programmes, other documents published pursuant to Community legislation, public contracts for food aid and the contents of the **OJ CE series.** The **OJ CE series** currently contains the preparatory acts in the legislative process (COM Documents) and is only available electronically on a monthly CD-ROM version or in the **EUR-Lex** (http://europa.eu.int/eur-lex/en/index.html) database (See European Union Web-sites section below for more details).

▶ **OJ S (Supplement) series** contains details of all public sector contracts for works, supplies and services from all the EU Institutions and EU Member States. The S series is **not** available in printed format. It is published as a daily or a twice-weekly CD-ROM.

> At present the <u>Official Journal</u> (http://europa.eu.int/eur-lex/en/search/search_oj.html) L and C series are available free and in full text (pdf format) on <u>EUR-Lex</u> (http://europa.eu.int/eur-lex/en/index.html) from 1998 onwards. Note, however, that legislative proposals appear in the **OJ CE** series, but without the key useful explanatory memorandum including in the original COM. The frequency of publication of the **OJ CE** series will depend on the frequency and volume of documents sent for publication by the EU institutions.
>
> The **Official Journal S (Supplement)** series is available on the <u>TED</u> (http://ted.eur-op.eu.int) database. In addition to current tenders, the TED database also gives easy access to an archive of the previous five years of the S series in English. Similar to the CD-ROM, a single search screen allows the user to select or to enter multiple search criteria, including geographical data, type of document, nature of contract, keywords and more. For more detail on the TED database see the European Union Databases section below.

Treaties

All primary legislation is contained in the various Treaties on which EU law is based. The Treaties assign specific roles and responsibilities to the various European institutions in the legislative process and provide the legal base for all subsequent legislation initiated by the various institutions. The Treaties also establish the procedure and processes through which legislative proposals must progress before they can be passed into law.

The European Union is based on the three founding treaties:

▶ the Treaty establishing the European Coal and Steel Community (ECSC), which was signed in Paris and entered into force on 23 July 1952,

▶ the Treaty establishing the European Community, which was signed in Rome and entered into force on 1 January 1958,

▶ the Treaty establishing the European Atomic Energy Community (Euratom), which was signed in Rome and entered into force on 1 January 1958.

These founding Treaties have been amended on several occasions, in particular on the accession of new Member States in 1973, 1981, 1986 and 1995. Three further Treaties have also been introduced to effect major institutional changes and establish new areas of responsibility for the European institutions:

▶ the Single European Act (SEA), which was signed in Luxembourg and The Hague and entered into force on 1 July 1987,

▶ the Treaty on European Union, which was signed in Maastricht and entered into force on 1 November 1993,

▶ the Treaty of Amsterdam, which entered into force on 1 May 1999.

The Treaty of Nice, agreed at the European Council on 7-9 December 2000 and signed on 26 February 2001, will make further amendments to the existing Treaties. The Treaty of Nice will enter into force once the 15 Member States, in accordance with their respective constitutional procedures, have ratified it.

The text of all EU Treaties are published in the *Official Journal of the European Communities L (Legislation) series* which is available in printed or CD-ROM format from the Office of Official Publications of the European Communities and on the Internet (see below).

The **Treaties** (http://europa.eu.int/eur-lex/en/search/search_treaties.html) section of the EU's legislative database **EUR-Lex** has full text versions of:

▶ the **Treaty of Nice** (http://europa.eu.int/eur-lex/en/treaties/dat/nice_treaty_ en.pdf) and a link to the **Treaty of Nice web-site** (http://europa.eu.int/comm/ nice_treaty/index_en.htm),

▶ consolidated versions incorporating the changes made by the Treaty of Amsterdam, signed on 2 October 1997, to the Treaty on European Union and the Treaty establishing the European Community,

▶ an electronic copy of the publication **Selected instruments taken from the Treaties** (http://europa.eu.int/eur-lex/en/treaties/dat/treaties_en.pdf), incorporating the provisions introduced by the Treaty of Amsterdam into both the **Treaty on European Union** and the **Treaty establishing the European Community** (http://europa.eu.int/eur-lex/en/treaties/dat/ec_cons_ treaty_en.pdf) . Please note that all of the publications on this web-site are in pdf format.

The ABC section on the Europa web-site also has a **Treaties** (http://europa.eu.int/abc/treaties_en.htm) page containing some Treaties in full-text pdf format. It also provides links to some Explanatory texts on the Amsterdam and Nice treaties.

COM Documents

The European Commission produces COM documents, the majority of which are proposals for future legislation. However, they are also the mechanism used to publish annual reports on Community programmes and general policy statements. These fall into five general headings:

▶ **Non-legislative communications** - documents which are sent by the Commission to one or more institutions and which are politically binding for the Commission in the future. They are forerunners of new programmes and have greater political weight than reports.

▶ **White papers** - documents containing proposals for Community action in a specific field

▶ **Green papers** - documents which are intended to stimulate discussion and initiate consultation at European level on a particular subject (e.g. social policy, telecommunications, legal aid, and environmental issues).

▶ **Reports** - the Commission drafts and publishes a whole range of sectoral reports on the application of various items of secondary legislation.

▶ **Commission working documents** - documents drawn up as a basis for debate in a specific field. They have less force than communications and are not politically binding for the Commission.

COM Documents are numbered sequentially each year and are quoted as, for example, COM (2000) 195.

COM Documents can be purchased individually or on standing order from the Office of Official Publications of the European Communities. The text of COM Documents is published in the *Official Journal of the European Communities C (Information and Notices) series*. Note that this is now only in the electronic version, **OJ CE** series in CD-ROM format from the Office of Official Publications of the European Communities and on the Internet (see below).

> The best internet source for those COM Documents which are legislative proposals is the **Legislation in Preparation** (http://europa.eu.int/eur-lex/en/com/index1.html) section of the EU's legislative database **EUR-Lex** (http://europa.eu.int/eur-lex/en/index.html). This provides free full-text to most of these documents but is limited to those that have neither completed the law-making procedure nor have been withdrawn from it.
>
> Users can access the legislative proposals in a number of ways:
> ▶ **The Analytical Register** (http://europa.eu.int/eur-lex/en/com/index.html) - a

listing of numerical classification codes taken from the *Directory of Community Legislation in Force*, divided into 20 chapters covering specific areas of Community activity.

▶ **Alphabetical Index** (http://europa.eu.int/eur-lex/en/com/abc/en_abc_index_01.html).

▶ **Search Engine** (http://europa.eu.int/eur-lex/en/search.html).

For more detailed information on how to use the search engine on the EUR-Lex database, please see European Union Web-sites section below.

Non-legislative COM Documents can be found in the **Documents of Public Interest** (http://europa.eu.int/eur-lex/en/search/search_dpi.html) section of **EUR-Lex** which can be searched by document type and then either chronologically or numerically.

At present the **Official Journal** (http://europa.eu.int/eur-lex/en/search/search_oj.html) L and C series are available free and in full text (pdf format) on **EUR-Lex** from 1998 onwards. Please note that legislative proposals appear in the electronic version of the **OJ CE** without the key useful explanatory memorandum included in the original COM. The frequency of publication of the **OJ CE** series will depend on the frequency and volume of documents sent for publication by the EU institutions.

Legislative materials

The legislative documents of the European Union, which are similar to UK and Scottish Acts of Parliament, may take one of four forms:

▶ **Regulations** - these are binding on all Member States and are directly applicable. Regulations do not require any additional action on the part of national governments and override any national legislation with which they might conflict. Regulations are mainly used for implementation of the Common Agricultural Policy (CAP). Regulations are referenced by running number, within a given year (e.g. Council Regulation (EC) 946/2001).

▶ **Directives** - these are binding on all Member States but permit national governments to introduce their own legislation interpreting the Directive within a given time period. In the UK and Scotland these may take the form of an Act or, more likely, a Statutory Instrument. Directives are also referenced by running number, however, the year comes first (e.g. Commission Directive 2001/32/EC).

▶ **Decisions** - these are binding only on those to whom they are addressed. They are usually directed at a named Member State or organisation and require specific action. Since 1992, Decisions have been given the same number sequence as Directives (e.g. Council Decision 2001/326/EC). It is very important to check whether the reference required is a Directive or a Decision.

▶ **Recommendations** - these are not binding but outline the opinions or position of the Community institutions on a topic. They are used mainly to promote the moral and political positions of the institutions.

The text of all Regulations, Directives, Decisions and Recommendations are published in the *Official Journal of the European Communities L (Legislation) series* which is available in printed or CD-ROM format from the Office of Official Publications of the European Communities and on the Internet (see below).

The best Internet sources for EU secondary legislation is the **Legislation** (http://europa.eu.int/eur-lex/en/search/search_lif.html) section of the EU's legislative database **EUR-Lex**. This provides free full-text access to Directives, Decisions and Regulations still in force. Information can be accessed in a number of ways:

▶ **The Analytical Register** (http://europa.eu.int/eur-lex/en/lif/index.html) - a listing of numerical classification codes taken from the *Directory of Community Legislation in Force* divided into 20 chapters covering specific areas of Community activity.

▶ **Alphabetical Index** (http://europa.eu.int/eur-lex/en/lif/abc/en_abc_index_ 01.html).

▶ **Search Engine** (http://europa.eu.int/eur-lex/en/search/search_lif.html).

For more detailed information on how to use the search engine on the EUR-Lex database, please see European Union Web-sites section below.

At present the **Official Journal** (http://europa.eu.int/eur-lex/en/search/search_ oj.html) L and C series are available free and in full text (pdf format) on **EUR-Lex** from 1998 onwards.

European Union web-sites and databases

In this section, some of the most important and widely used web-sites and databases will be described. This listing is selective and is based on experience of use. The sites are those considered likely to be useful to the general (rather than specialist) users of European information.

(http://europa.eu.int/index_en.htm)

The **Europa** (http://europa.eu.int/index_en.htm) web-site is the gateway to EU information on-line. From this portal, all the information made available on the Internet by the institutions and bodies of the European Union can be located. These include the European Parliament, the Council of the Union, the Commission, the Court of Justice, the Court of Auditors, the Economic and Social Committee, the Committee of the Regions, the European Central Bank and the European Investment Bank. Europa also provides a vast array of information on European integration, particularly concerning the European Union's objectives, policies and institutional set-up.

The web-site is divided into seven principal sections listed on the navigation bar on the left of the screen. When you place the cursor over any of the section headings, another box to the right of the navigation bar opens up with a series of sub-headings for each topic. By simply clicking on the required sub-heading , users are taken to the appropriate section of the Europa web-site (see below).

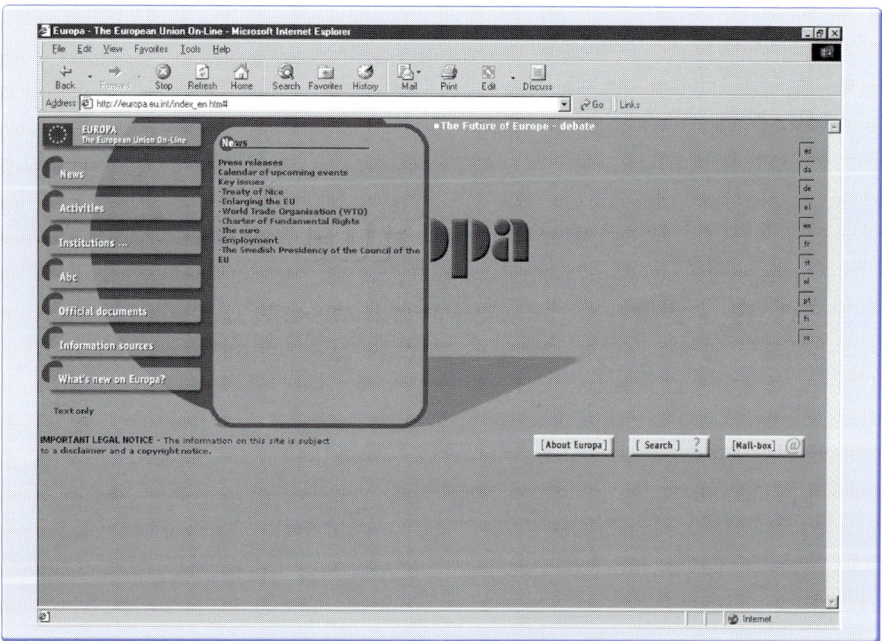

© European Communities, 1995-2001

A brief description of the contents of each section heading is listed below:

▶ **News** - this section is aimed principally at journalists and other people professionally involved in the information industry. It contains official press releases from the EU institutions and information on major forthcoming events.

- ▶ **Activities** sets out the Union's activities by subject (28 in total), giving an overview of the policies as well as more detailed information for students and professionals.

- ▶ **Institutions** provides a general introduction to each of the institutions as well as links to their home pages.

- ▶ **Abc** is aimed at the general public and sets out to provide clear answers to key questions concerning such things as the objectives of the European Union, European citizens' rights and the history of the EU.

- ▶ **Official documents** provides links to the major publications of the EU including the Official Journal, legislation and case-law.

- ▶ **Information sources** provides links to the major databases and information services available on the web, as well as direct links to the Office for Official Publications (OOPEC) and the Statistical Office of the EU (EUROSTAT).

- ▶ **What's new on Europa** provides a selection of news and the most recent additions to the Europa site and the sites of the other European institutions (launch of new sites, agenda of the institutions, official documents). This heading is updated daily. To access it, click on the 'What's New?' icon, which appears on all the Europa site pages.

There are also links to a **text-only** (http://europa.eu.int/index_ns_en.htm) version of the above pages which, in fact, functions as a site map and is a very useful place to start on Europa. In addition, the **About Europa** (http://europa.eu.int/abouteuropa/index_en.htm) section provides background information on the Europa service and there is also a **Search engine** (http://europa.eu.int/geninfo/query_en.htm).

Searching the Europa Web-site

Extensive advice on using the search engine can be found by clicking on the **Extended Help** (http://europa.eu.int/geninfo/search/index.htm) icon on the search screen. Users should scroll down this page until they come to the first of a series of help folders giving information and advice on how to search the Europa site effectively. Enter the word(s), or phrase(s) (phrase must be surrounded by double quotes e.g. "water pollution") into the text box and hit the search key under the text box. Boolean searching is also possible by linking search terms using the logical operators AND, OR, NOT.

A word of warning - Europa is a huge web-site and an unstructured search will retrieve literally thousands of hits. It is important that users do read the **help instructions** (http://europa.eu.int/geninfo/search/index.htm) before attempting to search the web-site.

Search

Europa

ES
DA
DE
EL
► EN ◄
FR
IT
NL
PT
FI
SV

News

Abc

Institutions

Policies

Formulate your query:

How to formulate your query?

- First aid: 5 basic search options
- Extended help: full search capabilities

Number of documents to display: 25 documents ▼

Retrieve only documents updated after: (date can be left blank) ____ (dd/mm/yyyy)

Document types:
○ Only HTML
◉ Multiple (HTML, PDF, Word, ...)

[Search] [Reset]

Some important databases on European affairs, accessible on Europa, are not retrievable via the query-box specified above

Note: Entering dd/mm/yyyy in the date-box (if it is not left blank) limits the search to those documents updated in Europa after the specified day, month and year.

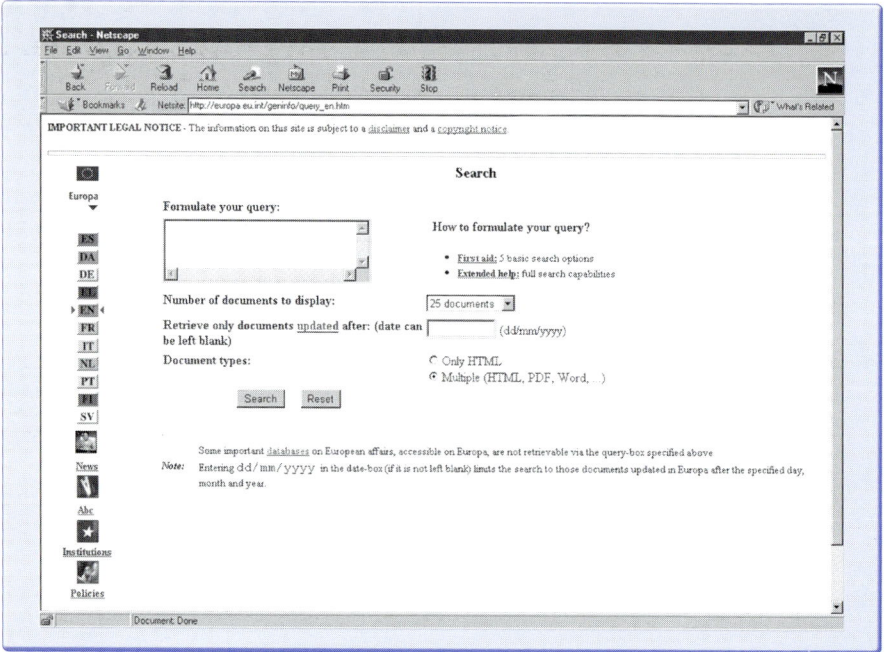

EUR-Lex
(http://europa.eu.int/eur-lex/en/index.html)

EUR-Lex , the portal to European Union law, is designed to keep citizens up to date on legislation in force in the European Union and new legislation as it is enacted. The EUR-Lex portal is a single entry access point to the complete collections of EU legal and judicial texts. Presently, the site has 6 general headings where users can select the 'latest' icon on the right of the screen to view the most recent additions or can search across all available documentation in each category.

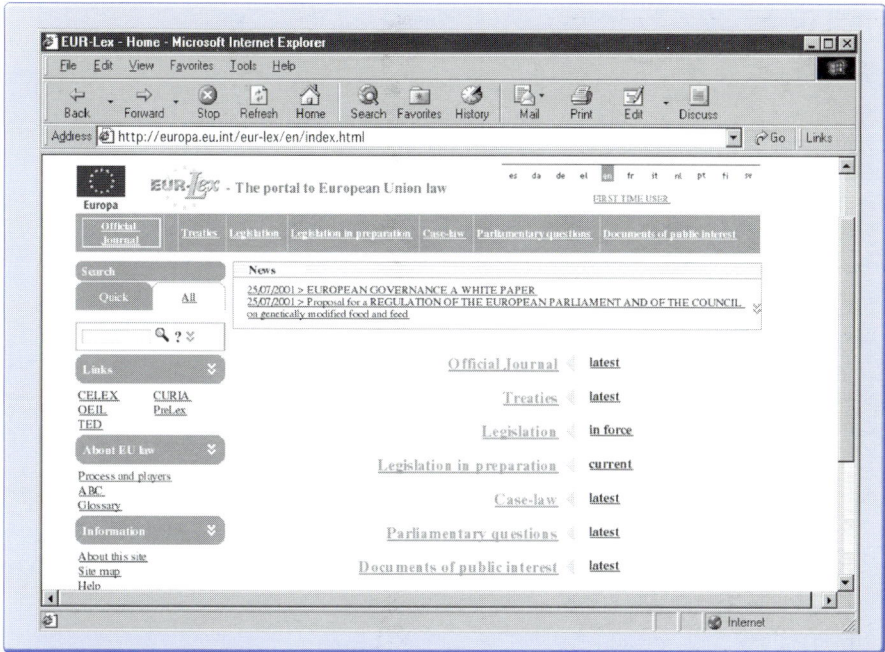

Presently, the 6 general headings of this site are:

▶ **The Official Journal** (http://europa.eu.int/eur-lex/en/search/search_oj.html) - At present both the L and C series are available free and in full text (pdf format) on **EUR-Lex** from 1998 onwards.

▶ **Treaties** (http://europa.eu.int/eur-lex/en/search/search_treaties.html) - full text (in pdf format) of the most important EU treaties.

▶ **Legislation** (Community Legislation in Force) (http://europa.eu.int/eur-lex/en/search/search_lif.html) - full text (some in pdf format) of all regulations, directives and decisions still in force.

▶ **Legislation in Preparation** (http://europa.eu.int/eur-lex/en/search/search_lip.html) - full-text (in pdf format) of most legislative COM documents but limited to those that have neither completed the law-making procedure nor have been withdrawn from it.

▶ **Case-Law** (http://europa.eu.int/eur-lex/en/search/search_case.html) - full-text of decisions and opinions of the Court of Justice of the European Communities, decisions of the Court of First Instance, and opinions of the Advocate General. For more information on this web-site, see Chapter 3.

▶ **Parliamentary Questions** (http://europa.eu.int/eur-lex/en/search/search_epq.html) - please note that Parliamentary Questions are not held on the EUR-Lex database. Clicking on this link will take users to the European Parliament web-site

▶ **Documents of Public Interest** (http://europa.eu.int/eur-lex/en/search/search_
dpi.html) - full text (pdf format) of the most important non-legislative COM
Documents.

Searching the EUR-Lex site

Users can search within each of the above categories - a dedicated search engine is
available on the home page of each particular category. Alternatively, a search can be
made across the whole EUR-Lex site by using the **search** (http://europa.eu.int/eur-lex/
en/search/index.html) facility. Please note that the EUR-Lex site has a very
comprehensive **search help** facility (http://europa.eu.int/eur-lex/en/information/help/
help_search.html). As in all searching, it helps greatly if the user reads the help guide.
Searches can be made by Document Number or by Word.

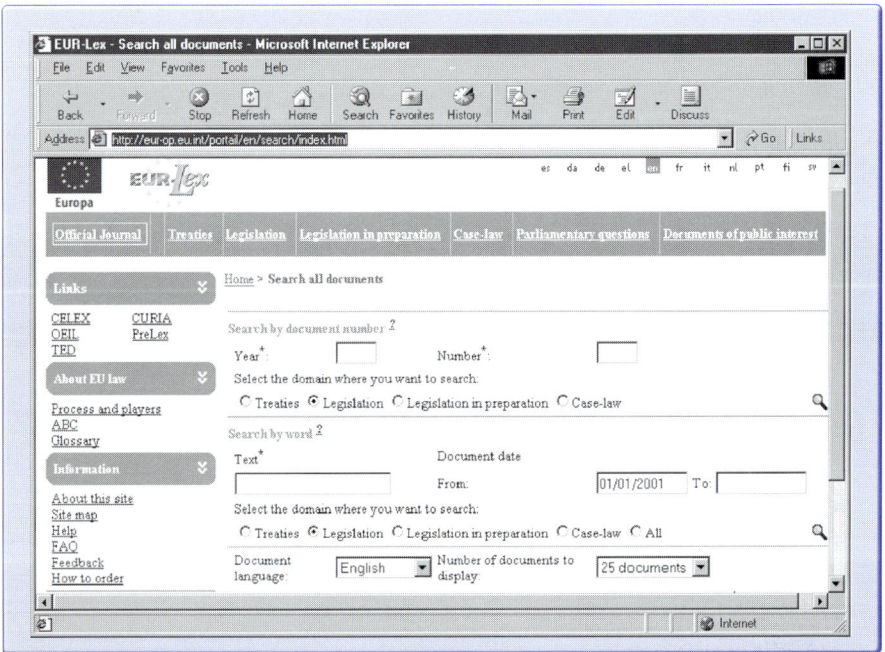

▶ **Document Number** - users can search by specific document number, using the
number allocated by the particular institution or publication (e.g. OJ publication
number, decision, directive, regulation number, COM series number) (see above).
Users must enter both the year of publication in four digits, (e.g. 1999) and the
document number. Please note that the domain default option on the Document
Number search option is always 'Legislation' - to change this, click on the option
of your choice. A search by document number returns a result page with the

documents found. The results page also includes a language bar option to repeat the search in that language.

▶ **Word** - The search engine allows plain text searching (see above) across the whole site or restricted to specific areas (e.g. Legislation) which can help limit and speed searches. Please note that the domain default on the Word search option is always 'Legislation' - to change this, click on the option of your choice. Enter the word(s), or phrase(s) (phrase must be surrounded by double quotes e.g. "water pollution") into the text box and hit the enter key, which is the magnifying glass icon at the far right of the screen. Boolean searching is also possible - when searching with a logical OR operator, the terms must be separated by a comma (e.g. legal, act will retrieve documents containing either legal or act or both) and when searching with a logical AND operator, the terms must be separated by a plus (e.g. legal+act will retrieve documents containing both legal and act terms). The search mechanism will return a result page with links to documents that match the words or phrases specified. Documents will be presented in order of relevance (most relevant documents at the top).

Please note that a **quick search** option is available on top left of the EUR-Lex home page.

TED Database
(http://ted.eur-op.eu.int/ojs/html/index2.htm)

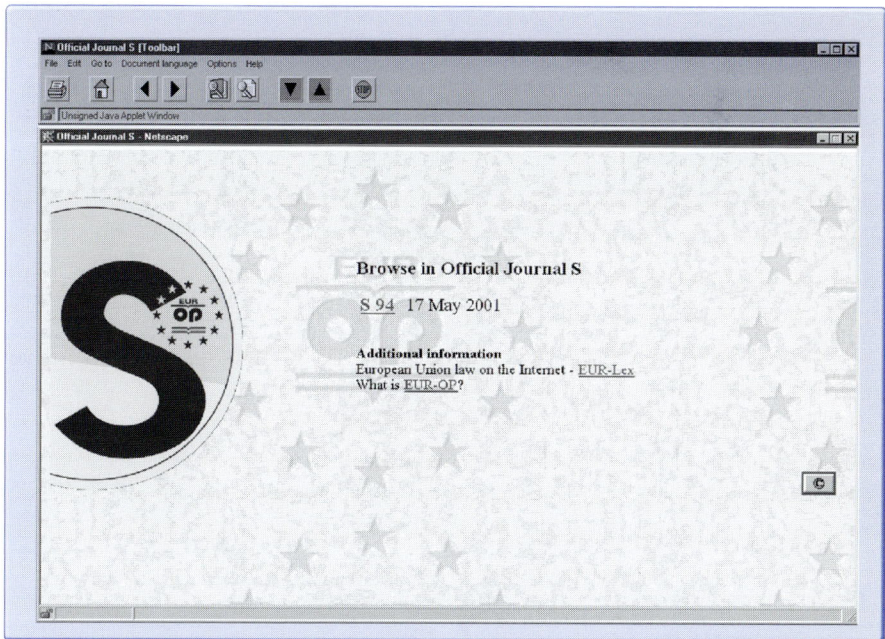

TED (Tenders Electronic Daily) (http://ted.eur-op.eu.int/ojs/html/index2.htm), the Internet version of the Supplement to the Official Journal of the European Communities (OJS), is a databank in which approximately 500 tender documents for public contracts issued by EU members states and Institutions are published daily. In addition to current tenders, the TED (http://ted.eur-op.eu.int/ojs/html/index2.htm), database also gives easy access to an archive of the previous five years of the S series in English. Please note that the recommended browser for using TED is Netscape 4.51, although it will work (with reduced functionality) on Internet Explorer.

Searching the TED Database

The toolbar at the top of the screen has a help (http://ted.eur-op.eu.int/ojs/en/help/ sail-ted.htm) icon directing users to detailed advice on how to search the TED database efficiently and effectively. As in all searching, it helps greatly if the user reads the help guide. Users can browse the daily edition of the database by clicking on the hypertext linked S Number on the home page (see above), or can search across the whole database by using a single search screen (accessible from the toolbar at the top of the screen). This allows the user to select or enter multiple search criteria, including geographical data, type of document, nature of contract, and keywords (see below). Note that users must click the search the archive box (previous 5 years) at the bottom of the search screen if they wish to look at the tender documents issued for public contracts in the previous five years.

© European Communities, 1995-2001

This section has discussed only a few of the European Union web-sites in detail. However, in the section on EU Institutions (above), the web addresses of each individual institution have been given. Users are also directed to the **European Databases on the Web** (http://www.lib.gla.ac.uk/Depts/MOPS/EU/databases.html) web-site at Glasgow University Library which provides a comprehensive and up to date listing of web-sites hosting free access to European Union databases.

Further EU Information Assistance in Scotland

Users seeking further information on the European Union and its publications can contact the four Scottish European Union Documentation Centres in:

Aberdeen: Taylor Library and European Documentation Centre, University of Aberdeen, Dunbar Street, Aberdeen AB24 3UB (http://www.abdn.ac.uk/~lib083/services/edc.html),

Dundee: European Documentation Centre, The Law Library, University of Dundee, Dundee DD1 4HN (http://www.dundee.ac.uk/edc/general.htm),

Edinburgh: Law and Europa Library, Old College, University of Edinburgh, South Bridge, Edinburgh EH8 9YL (http://www.lib.ed.ac.uk/lib/sites/law.shtml),

Glasgow: European Documentation Centre, Glasgow University Library, Hillhead Street, Glasgow G12 8QE (http://www.lib.gla.ac.uk/MOPS/EU/index.html).

Publications of other relevant public organisations and official bodies

T here is a wide range of public authorities, with varying degrees of administrative power, in Scotland. These include agencies, advisory bodies and what are described as 'Executive Non-Departmental Public Bodies'. This chapter seeks to list significant public bodies and web-sites that provide material that could be described as a publication, electronically and free of charge, regardless of type. For each location, the current address of the web-site is given, along with a description of the type of material to be found. This selection is, inevitably, selective but is based on experience of use and reliability. It concentrates on those organisations producing publications, or public information on a regular or occasional basis. As a consequence, some Executive Agencies of government (e.g. Historic Scotland) are listed while others (e.g. Scottish Public Pensions Agency) have been omitted.

In June 2001, the Scottish Executive announced that almost a third of Scotland's public bodies were to be abolished and a further sixty-one would be subject to a more fundamental review. The consultation paper **Public Bodies: Proposals for Change** (http://www.scotland.gov.uk/library3/government/pbreview.pdf) provides background to, and details of, the review. It is intended that fifty-two bodies will be abolished by May 2003 and further legislation will be introduced in September 2001 to deal with the remaining six bodies. Some of the public bodies earmarked for abolition or review are included in this chapter because they currently provide material in both printed and electronic formats but at the time of writing there has been no change in their status.

Many of these sites have very useful links to other national and international organisations and provide a good first step to accessing information in the relevant field. Sites that are specifically British, with no separate section for Scotland, have been mostly excluded as this is not intended to be a guide to all British sources and these are well described elsewhere. Where separate publications pages give access to electronic versions of printed material, the addresses have been given.

For some sites, an Adobe Acrobat reader is required to view the reports. If you require to install the reader on your machine, download the reader from the Adobe web-site, by clicking on the 'Get Acrobat' Reader image (http://www.adobe.co.uk/products/acrobat/readstep.html).

► **Audit Scotland** (http://www.audit-scotland.gov.uk/). Audit Scotland was set up in April 2000 to provide services to the Accounts Commission and the Auditor General for Scotland to ensure that the Scottish Executive and public sector bodies in Scotland are held to account for the proper, efficient and effective use of public funds. All of Audit Scotland publications are available in Acrobat format, including the Annual Report, an overview of local authority audits, performance indicators of the provision of council services, and audit reviews of such topics as National Health Service bodies in Tayside and the provision of pre-school education.

► **Commissioners of Northern Lighthouses** (http://www.nlb.org.uk/) – provides information on the Differential Global Positioning System (DGPS), a satellite based navigation aid provided by the three General Lighthouse Authorities of the UK and the Republic of Ireland. The web-site includes a chart of DGPS stations in the UK and Ireland, with their transmission frequencies. The site also links to the full details of *Notices to Mariners* on lights, buoys and fog signals.

► **Convention of Scottish Local Authorities (COSLA)** (http://www.cosla.gov.uk/) - links to news releases and briefings on issues relevant to local government in Scotland.

► **Deer Commission for Scotland** (http://www.dcs.gov.uk/). The Deer Commission is the non-departmental public body charged with furthering the conservation, control and management of all species of deer in Scotland. Under **publications** (http://www.dcs.gov.uk/htm/frames5.html), the site gives links to the Annual Report, other online documents (e.g. consultation and policy papers) and information on printed material.

► **Fisheries Research Services** (http://www.marlab.ac.uk/). An Agency of the Scottish Executive Environment and Rural Affairs Department, it comprises two fisheries laboratories for freshwater (Pitlochry) and marine (Aberdeen) fish and provides expert advice on fisheries, aquaculture and the aquatic environment. In addition to recent press information, the web-site links to a series of information sheets covering such subjects as shellfish and other species stocks, ocean climate, notifiable diseases in fish, and fishery management methods; under sea ice and pelagic surveys; ocean climate status reports; annual reports; fisheries research reports; information pamphlets; statistical bulletins and surveys of fish farms. A separate page has been created for downloading pdf files.

► **Forestry Commission** (http://www.forestry.gov.uk/). The Forestry Commission is the government department responsible for the protection and expansion of Britain's forests and woodlands. This site needs some tenacity to get to the available publications but it does provide links to published findings of individual research programmes (e.g. biodiversity, social forestry).

▶ **General Register Office, Scotland** (http://www.gro-scotland.gov.uk/grosweb/grosweb.nsf). The General Register Office for Scotland GRO(S) is the department responsible for the registration of births, marriages, deaths, divorces and adoptions in Scotland, and for carrying out the decennial censuses of Scotland's population. The site has links to a range of genealogical information, including **Scots Origins** (http://www.origins.net/GRO/) and searching historical sources for **Family Records** (http://www.gro-scotland.gov.uk/grosweb/grosweb.nsf/pages/famrec). For a fuller description of its statistical publications, see Chapter 7.

▶ **General Teaching Council for Scotland** (http://www.gtcs.org.uk/). The professional council for teaching in Scotland has a publications page, which links to online reports and policy documents (e.g. on guidance in secondary schools), as well as a list of other printed publications available from the Council. The site also has a small number of news releases with links to other relevant documents.

▶ **Health Education Board for Scotland** (http://www.hebs.scot.nhs.uk/). This site gives access to HEBSWEB, a comprehensive source of health education and health promotion resources, services and information for Scotland. The site is sub-divided into four key areas:

▶ **health topics**, which brings together a range of different information sources around each of the Board's priority health topics (e.g. alcohol misuse, cancer, oral health, physical activity), including information extracted from its data sets, relevant publications and more specific HEBSWEB resources,

▶ **services and resources**, which accesses key resources, including the full text of all HEBS **leaflets** (http://www.hebs.scot.nhs.uk/services/pubs/index.htm),

▶ **about HEBS** - information about the Board as an organisation, including **strategy and policy documents** (http://www.hebs.scot.nhs.uk/info/strategy/index.cfm) and **press releases** (http://www.hebs.scot.nhs.uk/info/press/index.cfm), as well as more detailed information about the **HEBSWEB** site itself,

▶ **specialist sub-sites**. The library specialist sub-site gives access to lists of new journal articles on health promotion and education (via the Health Promotion Library Scotland *Bulletin*) and links to other online publications, including the Annual Report.

▶ **HM Inspectorate of Education** (http://www.scotland.gov.uk/hmie/). An Agency of the Scottish Executive, HM Inspectors undertake independent and impartial evaluations of the quality of educational provision and publish reports on key aspects of education. Further education colleges are similarly reviewed. At present, only a small number of inspection reports are available on the site but there are links to other general publications produced by HMI, including its Standards and Quality, and Effective Learning and Teaching series, in addition to self evaluation and management documents.

▶ **Heritage Lottery Fund** (http://www.hlf.org.uk/). The Fund uses money raised by the National Lottery to safeguard and enhance heritage buildings and the environment. The site gives access to news releases (including Scotland as a chosen area), information on how to apply to the Fund, online versions of all **publications** (http://www.hlf.org.uk/pubfr.htm), reports of regional committee meetings, past grants and statistics on grants awarded and applications received.

▶ **Highlands and Islands Enterprise** (http://www.hie.co.uk/). The role of the Highlands and Islands Enterprise Network is to assist economic development within the Highlands and Islands. This very useful site has a valuable economic information section produced by its Economics Branch, with key statistics and economic reports on the region. Area updates review demographic and economic changes. Monthly digests, with analysis for Local Enterprise Company and travel-to-work areas, provide the most up-to-date information on unemployment in the area. There is also a business directory and a rural Scotland price survey, undertaken twice a year, giving information on the relative retail price of goods and services in various locations within the Highlands and Islands and other parts of Scotland. It is a useful indicator of the cost of living differentials within remote, rural and urban areas. These are published as downloadable pdf files. Finally, there is a link to the annual survey of Highland and Island exports which identifies sources, types, destinations and values.

▶ **Historic Scotland** (http://www.historic-scotland.gov.uk/sw-frame.htm). Historic Scotland is an Agency within the Scottish Executive Education Department and is responsible for safeguarding the nation's built heritage, and promoting its understanding and enjoyment. The Annual Report and Accounts, which is both a House of Commons and a Scottish Executive Paper, is available on this site. In addition, the site provides information about the carbon dating database (radiocarbon dates for archaeological sites issued before June 1996), a list of all staffed properties, a publications catalogue and press bulletins.

▶ **Law Society of Scotland** (http://www.lawscot.org.uk/). The Law Society of Scotland is the governing body for Scottish solicitors and provides services to the public in this field. See Chapter 3 on Scottish legal material for more details on the publications available from the Society.

▶ **Learning and Teaching Scotland** (http://www.LTScotland.com/). Formed by a merger of the Scottish Council for Educational Technology (SCET) and the Scottish Consultative Council on the Curriculum, LT Scotland aims to advise on the curriculum and the use of information and communications technology in education and in learning throughout life. It also seeks to develop products and services supportive of learning and teaching at all stages. The site is still being developed and, as yet, press releases appear to be the main information available. The site does link to:

- **SCET** (http://www.scet.com/home.asp) and, through it, to the **Scottish Virtual Teachers Centre** (http://www.svtc.org.uk/), part of the implementation of the National Grid for Learning in Scotland targeted at teachers and librarians who work in the Scottish early years and school sectors. It provides links to web-sites relevant to the Scottish curricula and to broad themes, resources contributed by practitioners, such as worksheets, assignments, and simulations, search options and a discussion area.

- **Scottish Consultative Council on the Curriculum** (http://www.sccc.ac.uk/home.html). In addition to the Annual Report, there are links to all the Scottish CCC **publications** that are currently available electronically (http://www.sccc.ac.uk/main/Publications/dwnld.html), in addition to two serial publications:

  - **Review**, a newsletter for teachers,

  - **5-14 Focus**, the newsletter of the Scottish Executive's national 5-14 Committee.

- **Macaulay Land Use Research Institute** (http://www.mluri.sari.ac.uk/). The principal Scottish land use research institute web-site has links to electronic versions of the Annual Report and newsletter, in addition to its **Economics and Policy Series** (http://www.mluri.sari.ac.uk/pub.htm).

- **Maritime and Coastguard Agency** (http://www.mcga.gov.uk/). The Agency is responsible for ensuring high standards of safety at sea and along the coasts, and minimising the risks of marine pollution. The site gives access to news releases, vessel detention lists, and maritime related prosecutions, seafarers standards, search and rescue operations, and policy on pollution prevention.

- **Moredun Research Institute** (http://www.mri.sari.ac.uk/). The Institute has an international reputation for its research into infectious diseases of sheep and other ruminants and the improvement of general animal health. Research is conducted in three divisions – bacteriology, parasitology and virology – and there are links to current research and relevant articles appearing in the Annual Reports.

- **National Archives of Scotland** (http://www.nas.gov.uk/). The National Archives is the repository for all the public and legal records of Scotland which are considered worthy of permanent preservation. It also holds many local and private archives dating from the 12th century to the present day. Its three buildings are in Edinburgh. Apart from the Annual Report, available in pdf format, there are links to descriptions of the various collections, information about exhibitions, their publications list, the Scottish Records Advisory Council (including the minutes of their last meeting) and the full text of various **fact-sheets** (http://www.nas.gov.uk/family_history_factsheet.htm).

▶ **National Board for Nursing, Midwifery and Health Visiting In Scotland** (http://www.nbs.org.uk/). This Board is the statutory body responsible for ensuring standards of education and training for nurses, midwives and health visitors in Scotland. It is accountable to government through the agency of the Management Executive for the National Health Service in Scotland. Press releases and agendas and minutes of Board meetings, in addition to Board responses to relevant policy documents and plans, can be accessed. There are links to other national nursing boards and commissioned research. At present, apart from the title *Providing Standards – Quality Assurance Handbook 2000*, none of its publications appear to be available electronically.

▶ **National Galleries of Scotland** (http://www.natgalscot.ac.uk/). This site gives access to information about the National Gallery of Scotland, the Scottish National Portrait Gallery, the Scottish National Gallery of Modern Art and the Dean Gallery, all in Edinburgh, and its two outliers in Banff and Paxton. Details about exhibitions, opening hours and publications lists for the individual institutions but relatively few images of works of art are available.

▶ **National Grid for Learning, Scotland** (http://www.ngflscotland.gov.uk/). The National Grid for Learning (NGfL) is part of a major Government initiative to connect all schools, colleges, universities and libraries to the Internet by 2002 and secure the benefits of advanced networked information technologies for all sectors of education and lifelong learning. In recognition of the educational, cultural and political differences between Scotland and the rest of the UK, the **NGfL Scotland team** was appointed. The background section of the site links to **Implementing the National Grid for Learning in Scotland** (http://www.scotland.gov.uk/library/documents-w/ngfl-00.htm), the full text of the Executive's plans for implementation. The site can be searched by subject, category topic (e.g. core skills, sport, world) and type. There is a section for parents, providing information about matters such as choosing a school, bullying and school quality, with links to relevant Scottish Executive publications, and another for teachers, the **Scottish Virtual Teachers Centre** (http://www.svtc.org.uk/) – see above.

▶ **National Library of Scotland** (http://www.nls.uk/). The National Library is the legal deposit library for Scotland and a general research library of international importance. It has an outstanding collection of books, manuscripts, maps and other material, much of which can be accessed from its online catalogues. There are links to news releases, the Annual Report and *Folio*, a journal highlighting collections, research and events at the Library.

▶ **National Museums of Scotland** (http://www.nms.ac.uk/). Links to the Royal Museum, the Museum of Scotland, the Museum of Flight, the Museum of Scottish

Country Life, the Museum of Costume and the National War Museum with information about the collections, exhibitions and products on sale at their shops.

▶ **National Trust for Scotland** (http://www.nts.org.uk/). Scotland's leading conservation charity concerned with both the natural and cultural heritage of the nation. In addition to news releases and a list of properties held in trust, there are links to information on conservation programmes.

▶ **Registers of Scotland** (http://www.ros.gov.uk/). The Executive Agency responsible for compiling and maintaining public registers relating to property and other judicial matters. The Land Register of Scotland and the Register of Sasines contain title information on all properties in Scotland, as well as ownership details, a description of the property (either verbal or by reference to a plan), the price paid and any outstanding securities (mortgages) which affect it. The Annual Report, which is a House of Commons and Scottish Executive Paper, is accessible from the site. There are also links to **Automated Registration of Title to Land (ARTL)** (http://www.ros.gov.uk/artlsite/index.html), a project to introduce paper-free registration of title to rights in land in Scotland and **Scotlis** (http://www.scotlis. com/), a project to provide integrated information about land and property from both private and public sectors.

▶ **Rowett Research Institute** (http://www.rri.sari.ac.uk/). The Rowett Research Institute is an independent charitable company substantially supported by grant-in-aid from the Scottish Executive Environment and Rural Affairs Department. It is involved in research on nutrition, and defining how it can prevent disease, improve health and enhance the quality of food production in agriculture. The site has information on its four research programmes – cellular integrity, nutrition and development, appetite and energy, and gut microbiology and immunology. In addition to the Institute's **Annual Report** (http://www.rri.sari.ac.uk/Publications. html), the site records a list of staff publications since 1977.

▶ **Royal Botanic Garden, Edinburgh** (http://www.rbge.org.uk/). The Garden is a scientific institution dedicated to high quality research on the systematics and biology of plants. The site provides information about the four gardens - Inverleith, Younger, Logan and Dawyck – and their collections. There is much detail about the scientific research carried out by staff, its education programme, a publications list (including other staff publications), and news releases. The catalogue of Living Collections and other plant databases can be searched.

▶ **Royal Commission on the Ancient and Historic Monuments of Scotland (RCAHMS)** (http://www.rcahms.gov.uk /). The Commission is an independent non-departmental government body financed under the sponsorship of Historic

Scotland. It carries out a programme of archaeological and architectural field surveys and recording of the built heritage of Scotland and makes this information available to the public through the Collections of the National Monuments Record of Scotland (NMRS), publication and exhibition of its work. The NMRS comprises a wide variety of indexed drawings, plans, photographs, printed material, maps, manuscripts and reports. The site includes a publications list, information on exhibitions, news items and a link to CANMORE (Computer Application for National Monuments Record Enquiries), providing on-line access to the NMRS database.

▶ **Royal Fine Art Commission for Scotland** (http://www.rfacs.com/). The Commission advises central and local government on the quality of the planning and design of the built environment, ranging from a single civic building to a large industrial complex set, from street furniture to the Skye Bridge. There are links to policy documents and the Commission's responses, and recent **case lists** (http://www.rfacs.com/case_main.htm) of expert comment on about one in every thousand planning applications.

▶ **Scotland Europa** (http://www.scotlandeuropa.com/). A Scottish Executive EU Office initiative to promote Scottish interests to the institutions of the EU. The site links to the full text of **Scotland Europa Papers** (http://www.scotlandeuropa.com/sp_index.htm), an occasional series contributing to key issues and a wider understanding of European issues in Scotland. There are also links to bodies seeking partnerships and to European regions and an extensive list of sites useful to those involved in Europe.

▶ **Scotland Research and Innovation** (http://www.cordis.lu/scotland/home.html). Providing information about Scotland's economy and development in a European context, this site provides access to a research and development funding database available to technology companies freely available on the Internet.

▶ **Scottish Agricultural Science Agency (SASA)** (http://www.sasa.gov.uk/default.htm). SASA is an Executive Agency and part of the Scottish Executive Environment and Rural Affairs Department (SEERAD). It provides expert advice on agricultural and horticultural crops and aspects of the environment, and is involved in work on plant health, bee health, variety registration, crop improvement and genetic resources. At present, there is very little in the way of publications on this site – the only item being a booklet on Crop production in the East of Scotland, available as a downloadable pdf file.

▶ **Scottish Archive Network (SCAN)** (http://www.scan.org.uk/). A three-year project aiming to link the catalogues of private and public archives of all sizes in Scotland in an electronic searchable network. Users will be able to search for material on individuals, organisations, businesses, and families and estates. In particular, the site will give free access to a comprehensive index of nearly half a million entries to the testaments (wills) of Scots recorded in the Registers of Testaments. There are guides to searching family history, some research tools (e.g. a guide to Scottish handwriting) and an on-line discussion forum for archivists and archive users.

▶ **Scottish Arts Council** (http://www.sac.org.uk/). The Council works to develop and promote the arts (crafts, dance, drama, literature and music) in Scotland. Key publications, newsletters and reports are available electronically. The site also links to a comprehensive collection of leaflets, fact-sheets, contact lists, and advice guides on the arts in Scotland. There are sections of the site devoted to SAC funding schemes and grants, and a poem and image of the month page.

▶ **Scottish Council for Research in Education** (http://www.scre.ac.uk/). SCRE is an independent national body which provides research, evaluation and training services under contract and expert gateways to educational research in Scotland. Much of this research is made available through its **publications** (http://www.scre.ac.uk/pubs/index.html) and a computerised database of Scottish educational research (**ERSDAT**) (http://www.scre.ac.uk/is/ersdat/index.html), covering the period since 1975. The site also includes the Annual Report, a newsletter, press releases, hypertext links to published current and recent research, and executive summaries of SCRE research reports. In addition, the site provides a **Teacher Researcher Support Network (STRSN)** (http://www.scre.ac.uk/tpr/index.html), research reviews (some available in full text) and **Spotlights** (briefing papers on various areas of educational research, again in full text and Acrobat format) (http://www.scre.ac.uk/spotlight/index.html).

▶ **Scottish Council for Voluntary Organisations** (http://www.scvo.org.uk/). The Council is the umbrella body for all voluntary organisations in Scotland. It promotes the independence, interests and values of the voluntary sector in the wider community and supports organisations to improve their effectiveness and capacity through providing access to training, information, analysis, funding opportunities and services. The site links to a publications catalogue, a policy archive of briefings and responses to relevant documents, information on its credit union, Social Inclusion Partnerships, the Older Industrial Areas Project and charity news.

▶ **Scottish Courts Service** (http://www.scotcourts.gov.uk/). This site provides access to information relating to all civil and criminal courts within Scotland and includes **Court Opinions** (http://www.scotcourts.gov.uk/pages/opinions_intro.htm), where the full text of the court opinions that have been published on the Internet can be viewed. See Chapter 3 on Scottish legal material for more details on the site.

▶ **Scottish Criminal Cases Review Commission** (http://www.sccrc.org.uk/). The Commission looks into alleged miscarriages of justice. See Chapter 3 on Scottish legal material for more details on this site.

▶ **Scottish Crop Research Institute** (http://www.scri.sari.ac.uk/). The Institute is a major international centre for research on important agricultural, horticultural and industrial crops and on the underlying processes common to all plants. It has nine research units, including cell biology and soil-plant dynamics, each with a series of research themes. The site provides information on these and other special topics, such as flatworms and soft fruit diseases and pests. Some of its many printed documents are available as downloadable pdf files, including recent press releases, leaflets and Annual Reports. One valuable aspect of this site to hard-pressed searchers is that it provides links to individual articles from the Annual Reports rather than having to download the entire Report.

▶ **Scottish Cultural Resources Access Network (SCRAN)** (http://www.scran.ac.uk/). SCRAN aims to create a fully searchable resource base of Scottish material culture and human history by working with museums, galleries, archives and universities to digitise selected parts of their collections. It is designed for education and provides access to thumbnail images of over half a million pages of history and culture, as well as brief, illustrated introductions to people, places, things, events and ideas with links to other relevant SCRAN resources.

▶ **Scottish Enterprise** (http://www.scottish-enterprise.com/). Scottish Enterprise is the main economic development agency for Scotland. With 12 Local Enterprise Companies, it works in partnership with the private and public sectors to develop and strengthen the Scottish economy by helping business, encouraging exports and attracting inward investment. Press releases, background information and profiles, as well as Annual Reports and Accounts of Scottish Enterprise and Local Enterprise Companies and research surveys (e.g. Scottish sales and exports) can also be accessed from the site. The site includes links to:

▶ **Locate in Scotland** (http://www.lis.org.uk/) – Scotland's inward investment agency, with links to information about key business sectors, its Annual Review and news bulletins.

▶ **Scottish Trade International** (http://www.scottish-enterprise.com/aboutscotland/trade/). The web-site of Scotland's international trade development agency provides links to its small business gateway and information about the Scottish economy, environment and trade.

▶ **Scottish Environment Protection Agency (SEPA)** (http://www.sepa.org.uk/). SEPA is the public body responsible for environmental protection in Scotland. It produces many reports on the environment, waste strategy, bathing waters and radioactivity. The site links to press releases, environmental data (including water quality, chemical emissions from large combustion plants and successful prosecutions), a wide range of policy documents and various information leaflets (http://www.sepa.org.uk/publications/index.htm). For more information on the statistical publications, see Chapter 7.

▶ **Scottish Further Education Funding Council** (http://www.sfefc.ac.uk/). The Council is the supporting body for further education in Scotland. The site provides access to the Annual Report, press releases, corporate publications, consultations, and circular letters (http://www.sfefc.ac.uk/library.htm). There are links to the web-sites of all Further Education Institutions funded by SFEFC.

▶ **Scottish Health on the Web** (http://www.show.scot.nhs.uk/). Hosted by the National Health Service in Scotland, this site provides a focal point for all NHS Scotland web-sites. It is very detailed and rather confusing but does allow access for both the public (which includes healthy living, NHS services and health advice) and NHS staff, as well as a guide to various other relevant national and support organisations. An extensive list of publications and consultation documents, many in Adobe Acrobat format, including those produced by Health Boards and those by the Information and Statistics Division, can be accessed (http://www.show.scot.nhs.uk/publications/pubindex.htm).

▶ **Scottish Higher Education Funding Council (SHEFC)** (http://www.shefc.ac.uk/). The Council provides financial support for teaching, research and associated activities in 18 Scottish higher education institutions. The usual range of Annual Reports, press releases, consultations and newsletters (http://www.shefc.ac.uk/publicat/intro.htm) is supplemented by links to:

▷ **Quality Assessment Reports by Subject** (http://www.shefc.ac.uk/publicat/qapubs/qareport.htm)

▷ **Quality Assessment Reports by Institution** (http://www.shefc.ac.uk/publicat/qapubs/insts/instlist.htm).

▶ **Scottish Homes** (http://www.scot-homes.gov.uk/). Scottish Homes is the national housing agency for Scotland. Working in partnership with local authorities, housing associations, the voluntary sector, private developers, economic development agencies, financial institutions and local communities, it seeks to help provide good housing and contribute to the regeneration of local communities. The site links to news releases, research reports and studies, and provides information on house condition surveys.

▶ **Scottish Law Commission** (http://www.scotlawcom.gov.uk/). The Commission's main task is to keep the law of Scotland under review and to recommend reforms which improve the law, simplify it and make it more accessible. See Chapter 3 on Scottish legal material for more details of this site.

▶ **Scottish Legal Aid Board** (http://www.scotlegalaid.gov.uk/). The Board is responsible for managing legal aid in Scotland, thereby allowing people who would not otherwise be able to afford it to have the help of a solicitor for their legal problems. See Chapter 3 on Scottish legal material for more details of this site.

▶ **Scottish Legal Services Ombudsman** (http://www.slso.org.uk/). The Ombudsman investigates complaints about the way in which a professional body has handled complaints against legal practitioners. See Chapter 3 on Scottish legal material for more details of this site.

▶ **Scottish Local Government Information Network** (http://www.slgiu.gov.uk/). This is the web-site of the Scottish Local Government Information Unit (SLGIU). As well as providing information about, and access to, its services, SLOGIN is a one-stop site with immediate access to all Scottish local government and other related web-sites. There are links to discussion papers, an electronic version of **Bulletin** (http://www.slgiu.gov.uk/bulletin/index.htm), the Unit's main vehicle for disseminating information about local government issues to councillors, member authorities, member trade unions and subscribers (most recent issue is November 1999), research and a publications list which includes the Directory of Scottish Local Government. However, much of its recent free material is not available electronically.

▶ **Scottish Natural Heritage** (http://www.snh.org.uk/). The remit of the organisation is to secure the conservation and enhancement of Scotland's wildlife, habitats and landscapes. The site gives access to its publications list, responses to government policy, the Annual Reports in downloadable format, statistics on the size and number of sites in each area, and descriptions of National Nature Reserves.

▶ **Scottish Police Forces Network** (http://www.scottish.police.uk/). This provides links to the eight Scottish police forces, the Annual Report of the Association of Chief Police Officers in Scotland, news, information on national campaigns and responses to relevant documents.

▶ **Scottish Policy Net** (http://www.scottishpolicynet.org.uk/). Hosted by Scottish Council Foundation which promotes independent thinking in public policy, this site seeks to provide a forum for policy discussion and strategic conversation about issues of critical significance to Scotland's future. It provides full texts of all the Foundation's **publications** (http://www.scottishpolicynet.org.uk/scf/publications/frameset.shtml) and gives details of the Foundation's work programme and current **research projects** (http://www.scottishpolicynet.org.uk/scf/projects/frameset.shtml).

▶ **Scottish Prison Service** (http://www.sps.gov.uk/). This is a clear and well laid out site providing information and statistics on the current prison population, the Annual Report (a House of Commons and SE Paper), news releases, all the research material published by the Research and Development Branch of the Scottish Prison Service, including the Occasional Papers series and prison surveys, information on individual prisons and current publications.

▶ **Scottish Qualifications Authority** (http://www.sqa.org.uk/). SQA is the national body in Scotland responsible for the development, accreditation, assessment, and certification of qualifications other than degrees. The site provides statistics on qualifications offered or accredited by it, covering uptake, attainment and the characteristics of candidates. The original tables, in Microsoft Excel 97 format, can be downloaded to enable further analysis. The site also gives access to specimen question papers, course material and a publications list.

▶ **Scottish Unitary Authorities** (http://www.trp.dundee.ac.uk/data/councils/stats.html). Hosted by the University of Dundee, Town and Regional Planning Department, this site has a clickable map of council areas and former administrative areas, as well as lists of main towns and islands and certain, now dated, key statistics.

▶ **sportscotland** (http://www.sportscotland.org.uk/). The national agency dedicated to promoting sporting opportunities for all Scots at all levels, regardless of interest and ability. In addition to the Annual Report, Council Minutes and news releases, the site provides information about funding and sponsorship, national centres, policy documents, and a publications catalogue with more recent **research reports** and **digests** (http://www.sportscotland.org.uk/contents/publications/research/researchsummaries.htm) available to download in pdf format.

▶ **visitscotland** (http://www.visitscotland.com/). The web-site of the body responsible for tourism in Scotland, it has links to transport (including timetables), general guides, accommodation, outdoor activities and the Scottish Convention Bureau (promoting Scotland as a destination for conferences).

Scottish Political Parties on the Web

▶ **Scottish Conservative and Unionist Party** (http://www.ScottishTories.org.uk/). Press releases, election manifestos, policy information, links to MSPs and MEPs, and a list of local councillors are available from this site.

▶ **Scottish Labour Party** (http://www.scottishlabour.org.uk/). Links to recent news releases and briefings, consultative policy documents and briefings (as well as information on policy making), and elected party representatives in national and local government.

▶ **Scottish Liberal Democrats** (http://www.scotlibdems.org.uk/). News releases, a list of prospective parliamentary candidates, a record of European, Westminster, Scottish and local by-elections, links to elected members in the various levels of national and local government, local parties and associated organisations, policy documents and conference motions are all accessible from the site.

▶ **Scottish National Party** (http://www.snp.org/). The site provides access to news releases, local associations, SNP parliamentarians and policy statements on employment, education, crime and health.

▶ **Scottish Green Party** (http://www.scottishgreens.org.uk/). Access to news bulletins, briefings, information on the party, policy pointers (short introductions to policies in such matters as agriculture, transport, language and culture, and drugs), election manifestos, its political principles (available in English, Gaelic and Scots), and key members of the party.

▶ **Scottish Socialist Party** (http://www.scottishsocialistparty.org/homepage.htm). The site provides information on the party, links to decisions taken at the annual conference, Voice (http://www.scottishsocialistvoice.net/index.html) (an online version of the party's newspaper), international issues, the Socialist Cultural Network, local branches, news items, election campaign details and results, and the party manifesto.

7 Chapter

Scottish Statistics

Ome very important element within the field of Official Publications is the production of official statistics on all aspects of society. Increasingly, government departments and other bodies rely on statistics to support planning in the provision of services and to identify areas of need. This chapter will consider statistical material emanating from the wide range of official bodies producing relevant data for Scotland. One of the most significant consequences of devolved government has been the marked increase in the publication and availability of figures about many aspects of Scottish life. A considerable proportion of the relevant statistics is created by, or for, the Scottish Executive. These will be considered first. However, it is very important to stress that Scotland sits within the United Kingdom and the European Union. Statistical material produced at these levels can often be relevant and will also be discussed.

There are a great many specialist publications with detailed statistics on quite specific topics. In this chapter, only the most useful, general compilations under specific subjects will be considered. Once again, users should be aware that statistical material, like other forms of official publications, tends to come in two formats – printed and electronic. In the case of statistics, the term 'electronic' covers a range of media including on-line datasets, CD-ROM and the Internet. The frequency of publishing statistics varies from the 'one-off' comprehensive investigation (e.g. **Trends in Cancer Survival in Scotland 1971-1995** (http://www.show.scot.nhs.uk/isd/Scottish_Health_Statistics/ subject/Cancer_survival/trends_1971-95.pdf) published by the Information and Statistics Division of NHS Scotland) to the regular bulletins and serial publications (e.g. **Scottish Social Statistics** (http://www.scotland.gov.uk/stats/sss/sss-00.asp)).

As with other aspects of Official Publications, certain material is only available in electronic format and this will be highlighted. Electronic publishing of statistical material poses a serious problem of bibliographical control since the individual publications can be treated as 'one-off' items and not part of a series. Where irregular statistical bulletins are discussed, web addresses have **not** been provided, as these may be superseded by more recent figures. Annual publications (including annual bulletins) will be given the web-address of the most recent issue at time of writing.

In this section, all of the major providers and their key publications are discussed. An arrangement by agency has been used for printed material because of the diversity of publication but this provides only a select list of the most useful general titles published by each of the key agencies. It is assumed that readers are likely to be more interested in sources arranged by subject or theme than by agency. In consequence, the web sources are grouped by the five key themes identified on the **Statistics in the Scottish Executive web-site** (http://www.scotland.gov.uk/stats) and that is where users will find a more detailed consideration of the wide range of statistics available.

Scottish Executive

The Scottish Executive has its own Statistical Service that provides Parliament, government and the community in general with information, analysis and advice on many aspects of Scottish life. Relevant publications produced by the Scottish Office prior to devolution are also considered in this section. Statistical material is available in a variety of paper forms and on the **Statistics in the Scottish Executive web-site**. Many of the Executive's statistical outputs contribute to the UK National Statistics (see below) and there is a particular Minister, the Minister for Finance and Local Government, with overall responsibility for statistics in the Executive. In April 2000, the Executive published its **Statistical Plan 2000-2001** (http://www.scotland.gov.uk/consultations/sesp-00.asp) as a consultation document, allowing users to comment on the priorities for developing statistics in the following year.

The **Statistics in the Scottish Executive web-site** contains all Executive statistical publications free of charge and has a well-developed **search engine** (http://www.scotland.gov.uk/stats/) that allows users to search for statistics on a specific topic under five thematic headings:

▶ **General Statistics**, which include background, reference and compendia figures,

▶ **Economy**, which is sub-divided into the economy, commerce, energy and industry, and the labour market,

▶ **People**, which is sub-divided into social and welfare, health and care, population and migration, education and training, and housing,

▶ **State**, sub-divided into crime and justice, and other government,

▶ **Land**, sub-divided into environment, transport, travel and tourism, and agriculture and fisheries.

The statistics themselves are grouped by type - sources, publications, analyses or datasets. Frequently, there are links to external (i.e. non-Scottish Executive) web-sites.

The **Statistics in the Scottish Executive web-site** homepage also provides links to:

▶ new and forthcoming statistical releases, indicating title, publication date and format (i.e. whether the publication is a compendium, a news release, a statistical bulletin or a separate publication),

▶ other government departments issuing statistics (arranged under the same five thematic headings),

▶ **StatBase** (http://www.statistics.gov.uk/statbase/mainmenu.asp), the on-line database of National Statistics (see below), which holds a large selection of Government statistics,

▶ a list of contact names and telephone numbers for statistics on a wide range of subject areas in the Executive.

While individual departments within the Executive have their own statistical units, information can be provided to the Scottish Executive by other government agencies and departments; for example, the General Register Office for Scotland provides the Scottish Executive and local authorities with statistical information about population size and structure. Local authorities and health boards also collect statistics on the services they provide that are used by the Executive.

Based on experience of use, the major printed serial publications currently emanating from the Scottish Executive are: **Scottish Economic Statistics** (http://www.scotland.gov.uk/stats/ses2001/ses-00.asp) and **Scottish Social Statistics** (http://www.scotland.gov.uk/stats/sss/sss-00.asp). Between them, they cover the range of information formerly presented in the *Scottish Abstract of Statistics*, which had been the definitive statistical publication of the Scottish Office from 1971 to 1998.

▶ *Scottish Economic Statistics* is published annually and provides a comprehensive range of official information on the Scottish economy. This includes macroeconomic indicators, including gross domestic product (GDP), data on the industrial sectors, household income and expenditure, and the labour market. The printed version is published as a Scottish Executive Paper and will have a different SE number (rather than a series number) for each issue. It is supplemented twice a year by *Scottish Economic Report*. This is a useful publication because it provides commentary on the relevant data and sets the Scottish economy in a wider context. Both these publications replace *Scottish Economic Bulletin*, which for almost thirty years had been the primary source of information on the economy of Scotland.

The Scottish Parliament Information Centre (SPICe) has produced a valuable guide to key sources of data on the Scottish economy. **Sources of Statistics on the Scottish Economy** (http://www.scottish.parliament.uk/whats_happening/research/pdf_subj_maps/smda00-01.pdf) is available in electronic format only from the Scottish Parliament web-site.

▶ *Scottish Social Statistics* is an entirely new compendium publication providing a broad picture of contemporary society in Scotland. It is similar in style to *Social Trends* (see National Statistics), using a mixture of text, charts and tables to cover the same key policy areas. The printed version will not be published on an annual basis as many aspects of social conditions change only slowly over time. However, a range of bulletins, news releases and one-off publications, in particular themed reports, will supplement it. Readers should be aware that the web version will contain the most up-to-date figures as they become available. At the end of each chapter there is a reference section containing useful reference web-sites, contact details for the chapter author and key providers of data. The printed version is published as a Scottish Executive Paper and will have a different SE number (rather than a series number) for each issue.

There are many other important printed titles of which users should be aware. As these are general in their approach and content, and likely to be held by major reference libraries, this selective list is arranged alphabetically by title. The electronic versions of these publications will be discussed in greater detail at a later stage in this chapter.

▶ **Annual Expenditure Report** – basically, the budgetary spending plans of the Scottish administration, set out by portfolio.

▶ **Economic Report on Scottish Agriculture** – an annual report providing provisional estimates of agricultural output, input and income for Scotland. The tables are accompanied by commentary and include figures on financial results by type of farming, land use, livestock, labour and farm type.

▶ **Scotland's People: results from the Scottish Household Survey** – published annually, it provides detailed results from the Survey about people living in Scotland today. It covers such characteristics as household behaviour relating to transport, social inclusion and public services. It is supplemented by the quarterly **Scottish Household Survey Bulletin**.

▶ **Scottish Community Care Statistics** – a new series of annual compilations of statistics from a wide range of health and social care services for adults in Scotland based on services provided rather than the people receiving services.

▶ **Scottish Crime Survey (SCS)** - a large-scale household survey of public experiences and perceptions of crime, based on interviews with over 5,000 adults across Scotland. The SCS is conducted approximately every four years, with the last sweep having been completed in 2000. Summaries of research findings are available from the Scottish Executive's Central Research Unit.

▶ **Scottish Environment Statistics** – appears irregularly but is an essential compilation of statistics on environmental topics such as land, atmosphere, water, conservation, radioactivity and recreation.

▶ **Scottish Health Surveys** – an irregular survey published as a monograph report which aims to monitor trends in health, to identify risk factors associated with particular health conditions, to consider differences between regions and subgroups of the population, and to enable comparison with England. This is a sample survey based on 13,000 Scots living in private households. It contains information on such topics as long-standing illness, use of health services, physical activity, eating habits and smoking and drinking.

▶ **Scottish Local Government Financial Statistics** – an annual series of tables largely relating to local authority accounts, including employment and taxation. The majority of the tables are arranged by sector (e.g. roads and transport, social work) and not by authority. This is now issued as a Scottish Executive Paper and will have a different SE number (rather than a series number) for each issue.

▶ **Scottish Transport Statistics** –an annual publication offering a wide variety of information on motor vehicles, bus and coach travel, toll bridges, air and shipping services. It is strong on showing trends over time and provides comparisons with figures for the UK as a whole.

At the time of writing, there no single, comprehensive printed volume of education statistics for Scotland. HM Inspectors of Schools publish a series of Annual Information Reports on Schools (AIRS) from data supplied by the Scottish Executive Education Department. These are:

▶ **Attendance and Absence in Scottish Schools**
▶ **Examination Results in Scottish Schools**
▶ **Leaver Destinations from Scottish Secondary Schools**
▶ **Scottish Schools: Costs.**

Increasingly, education statistics will be disseminated electronically by news releases, with accompanying tables, through the Scottish Executive web-site.

Pre-Devolution Statistical Material from Scottish Office Sources

The majority of statistical publications which emanated from the Scottish Office have continued in either the same form or under a slightly different title. The two principal works, which have not been continued since devolution, are:

▶ **Scottish Abstract of Statistics** - from 1971 to 1998, it was the major reference volume for statistics on all aspects of life in Scotland. Many of the tables showed series for a number of years whilst others provided information at local authority level.

▶ **Scottish Economic Bulletin** – from 1971 to 1999, this twice yearly bulletin from the Education and Industry Department included a review of the UK and Scottish economies. It provided an indication of trends as well as an extensive index of charts and statistics on such topics as output, personal/household income and expenditure, the business sector and the labour market.

The Scottish Office also produced a varied range of statistical bulletins on social work, housing, education, industry, agriculture, environment, transport and criminal justice. Many of these have continued under the Scottish Executive.

Although the Scottish Executive is the major source of many statistics, there are several other bodies in Scotland producing significant material. In particular, the **General Register Office for Scotland** (http://www.gro-scotland.gov.uk) and the **Information and Statistics Division of NHS Scotland** (http://www.show.scot.nhs.uk/isd/) produce multiple datasets across a wide range of topics. Other Scottish public sector bodies (e.g. **Scottish Environmental Protection Agency (SEPA)** (http://www.sepa.org.uk/) and **Scottish Higher Education Funding Council (SHEFC)** (http://www.shefc.ac.uk/) also publish statistics. There is no one comprehensive source for all statistical material produced in Scotland but users are directed to the **Scottish Statistics** (http://www.gla.ac.uk/Library/Depts/MOPS/Offpub/scotstat.html) web-site at Glasgow University Library which aims to cover all the most important sources.

General Register Office for Scotland

The General Register Office for Scotland (GRO(S)) is a department of the Scottish Executive. It is the Office of the Registrar-General for Scotland, who has responsibility for civil registration (births, deaths, marriages, divorces and adoptions) and the taking of censuses. The main printed statistical publications of the General Register Office for Scotland are:

▶ **Annual Report of the Registrar-General for Scotland** - contains commentary and detailed tabular information on population, births, deaths, cause of death, stillbirths and infant deaths, marriages, divorces and other related topics. The printed version is published as a Scottish Executive Paper and will have a different SE number (rather than a series number) for each issue.

▶ **Mid-Year Population Estimates** - produced annually and relate to 30 June of the relevant year. They are generally released during April of the following year.

▶ **Population Projections** - prepared at regular intervals by the Government Actuary's Department in consultation with GRO(S).

▶ **Census Publications** - a vast amount of population and socio-economic information is published in paper and electronic formats from the decennial census. This is produced in an extensive series of volumes of tables and reports presented as national and regional figures on all topics covered by the Census.

▶ **Electoral Statistics** - provides statistics about the number of electors by region, council area or constituency for the Scottish, Westminster and European Parliaments and local government.

Information and Statistics Division of the NHS Scotland

The major serial publications currently published by the Information and Statistics Division (ISD) are:

▶ **Scottish Health Statistics** - an annual publication presenting the latest available data and trend statistics on a comprehensive range of health topics covering health, morbidity, mortality, lifestyle and deprivation. Note, however, that from 2000 onwards the full edition of Scottish Health Statistics appears on the web only while a short summary print volume is available on request from the ISD.

▶ **Scottish Health Service Costs** - an annual publication providing information on expenditure incurred by the Health Service and the cost of providing particular health services (e.g. maternity services, psychiatric services). Most of the information relates to individual hospitals.

Scottish Centre for Infection and Environmental Health (SCIEH)

The Scottish Centre for Infection and Environmental Health (SCIEH) is responsible for the national surveillance of communicable diseases and environmental health hazards. It produces two significant printed serial publications:

▶ **Review of Communicable Diseases in Scotland** - an annual publication which contains data on communicable diseases, including data on immunisation and vaccine preventable diseases, respiratory infections and meningitis, travel health, sexually transmitted infections, HIV infection and AIDS, hepatitis b and c, methicillin resistant staphylococcus aureus and gastro-intestinal infections.

▶ **SCIEH Weekly Report** – this regular publication incorporates AIDS News Supplement (ANSWER) and contains epidemiological data on sexually transmitted infections, HIV infection and AIDS, hepatitis b and c, methicillin resistant staphylococcus aureus and gastro-intestinal infections.

Scottish Environmental Protection Agency (SEPA)

The Scottish Environmental Protection Agency is the public body responsible for environmental protection in Scotland and it produces a range of reports, many of which include statistical material. Key titles with statistics from SEPA are:

▶ **Radioactivity in Food and the Environment** - an annual report on radiological surveillance programmes with many tables, graphs and maps.

▶ **Scottish Bathing Waters Report** - an annual report providing comprehensive information on Scotland's coastal and inland bathing waters, again with many graphs, charts and figures.

▶ **State of the Environment Reports**   first published in 1996 as an initial attempt to provide a national overview of Scotland's environment, this has subsequently been updated by a series of topic reports on Water (1999), Air (2000) and Soil (2001).

Scottish Homes

Scottish Homes is the national housing agency for Scotland. It produces:

▶ **Scottish House Condition Survey** - the largest individual housing research project in Scotland. It has been conducted on two occasions to date, in 1991 and 1996, with a third survey scheduled to take place in 2002. The main report of the Scottish House Condition Survey 1996 was published in October 1997 and there is a continuing programme of analysis being carried out within and outwith Scottish Homes.

Scottish Parliament

Frequently, Written Answers to Parliamentary questions provide much detail on all aspects of policy.

▶ **Written Answers Report** - a very useful source of statistical information across a range of topics. Answers often provide details on costs and figures which may not always be available elsewhere (e.g. the number of convictions for the supply of drugs by each sheriff court in each year, 1987-99 - S1W-14157; answer in Written Answers, vol.11, no.5, p.308-309). See Chapter 1 for more information.

Sources from outwith Scotland

National Statistics

The United Kingdom National Statistics agency groups its publications under the following broad subject headings (themes):
Agriculture, Fishing and Forestry, Other Government, Commerce, Energy and Industry, Health and Care, Compendia and Reference, Labour Market, Crime and Justice, Population and Migration, Economy, Social and Welfare, Education and Training, Transport, Travel and Tourism, and the Natural and Built Environment. The major relevant printed sources containing figures for Scotland are:

▶ **Annual Abstract of Statistics** - the principal printed statistical yearbook for the United Kingdom. It contains a comprehensive collection of statistics covering all aspects of national life and the most recent volume includes specific tables for

Scotland on hospital and primary care services, crimes and penal establishments, and local authority income and expenditure.

▶ **Education and Training Statistics for the United Kingdom** - the primary source of education and training statistics for the UK as a whole, providing an integrated overview in over 50 tables. Many of the tables allow comparisons to be made over time and also between the four countries.

▶ **Labour Force Survey** - a continuous sample survey providing information about the United Kingdom labour force. Sub-national economic regions are included.

▶ **Regional Trends** - provides a unique description of the regions of the United Kingdom across a wide diversity of topics. Some tables are broken down into the sub-regions of Scotland.

▶ **Social Trends** - draws together social and economic data to paint a broad picture of contemporary British society. It is designed as a non-technical reference source aimed at a wide audience. Some tables compare Scotland with England and Wales, and Ireland.

▶ **Transport Statistics Great Britain** - compiled by the staff of Transport Statistics, with contributions from the Scottish Executive, the Welsh Assembly and other Government Departments. It contains statistical information concerning all aspects of transport in Great Britain, with figures for Scotland at a national level.

Statistical Office of the European Communities (EUROSTAT)

Eurostat is the Statistical Office of the European Communities situated in Luxembourg. Its task is to provide the European Union with statistics at European level that enable comparisons between countries and regions. Eurostat's principle printed publications containing information at a regional level (which, for Scotland, is the division into North Eastern Scotland, Eastern Scotland, South-western Scotland, and the Highlands and Islands) are:

▶ **Demographic Statistics** - all the principal series of demographic statistics are covered, namely population by sex and age group, births, deaths, migration, marriages, divorces, fertility, life expectancy and population projections. Both absolute numbers and rates are given in considerable detail for each country in the Union and also for EFTA members and a number of other European countries. While most tables provide detail at national level, there are several tables which provide indicators at a regional level.

▶ **Labour Force Survey** - presents the detailed results of the survey conducted in the Member States of the European Union. Data covered includes: the labour force and unemployed persons by sex and age group; employed persons by sex, professional status and branch of activity; weekly working hours; the main groups of persons seeking employment, by sex, reason for seeking employment, duration of search and methods used. While most tables provide detail at national level, at the end of each chapter there is a table showing the main indicators at a regional level.

▶ **Regions Statistical Yearbook** - gives the latest statistics relating to economic and social factors in the regions of the European Union. This includes population, employment and unemployment, the economy, agriculture, industry, energy, services and research and development. The publication contains a CD-ROM providing access to the latest available year's data from the REGIO database.

At present, the Eurostat and European Environment Agency web-sites have very little data available at the Scottish level and much is provided only on a subscription basis.

The majority of these printed publications are available from **The Stationery Office** (http://www.clicktso.com/) or by enquiry through the individual responsible body.

Statistics on the Web

In this section, web sources are grouped by the five key themes identified on the **Statistics in the Scottish Executive web-site** (http://www.scotland.gov.uk/stats): General, Economy, People, State and Land. The web-sites of other key statistical agencies who make their data available via the Internet will be highlighted under each heading as appropriate.

The **Statistics in the Scottish Executive web-site** (http://www.scotland.gov.uk/stats/) is arranged by the thematic headings (pillars) used by the Government Statistical Service (GSS). Each theme has its own web-page and you can find information about that general subject area by using the 'Whole Pillar' bar at the top of each page. Information is further sub-divided into topic areas and type - Sources, Publications, Analyses or Databases - although, at present, there appears to be little in the latter two sections. Users can search the 'Whole Pillar' by type or go directly to the topic listed below the 'Whole Pillar' bar and find links to statistics listed under databases, publications, sources and, where available, analyses.

Users can also search the whole **Statistics in the Scottish Executive web-site** (http://www.scotland.gov.uk/stats/) site by using the 'search for' option on the home page. At present, the search engine does not appear to be particularly sophisticated and seems to produce only word in title results. For example, publications are retrieved for a search on 'domestic abuse' but not for 'domestic violence'. Boolean searching does **not** appear to improve the results.

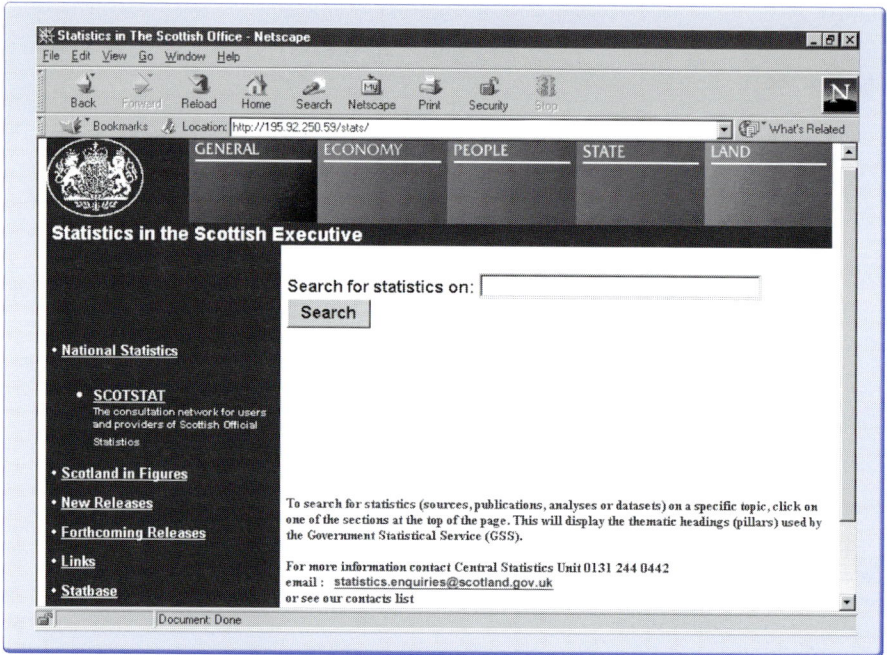

General Statistics

(http://www.scotland.gov.uk/stats/general.htm)

▶ **Background** (http://www.scotland.gov.uk/stats/stat-search.asp?pillar=general&key =scot) - links to a number of key publications and guides produced in Scotland including:

▶ **Scottish Economic Statistics** (http://www.scotland.gov.uk/stats/ses2001/ses-00.asp) - an electronic version of the annually printed publication. It provides a comprehensive range of official information on the Scottish economy.

▶ **Scottish Social Statistics** (http://www.scotland.gov.uk/stats/sss/sss-00.asp) - contains a whole range of statistics on contemporary Scottish society. The Scottish Social Statistics web-site contains some interactive elements and it is intended that, over time, the web version will be added to, as more information becomes available.

▶ **Scottish Statistics** (http://www.scotland.gov.uk/library2/doc16/ss2-00.asp) - a web only publication, produced by the Scottish Executive in 2000, containing statistics across a range of topics but without much detail.

▶ **Reference and compendia** (http://www.scotland.gov.uk/stats/stat-search.asp?pillar= general&key=scot) - presently, this appears to contain exactly the same information as Background.

Other useful web-sites containing general statistical material

▶   **Scottish Parliament** (http://www.scottish.parliament.uk/)

▶   **The Written Answers Report**
(http://www.scottish.parliament.uk/official_report/pq.html) is a very useful source
of statistical information across a wide range of topics. At the top of the page are
links to the Daily Written Answers, these appear only on the web, and are produced
in advance of the Written Answers Report which is published weekly. **The Written
Answers Report** has no index. However, it is possible to locate written answers on
a particular topic by using the Scottish Parliament web-site **search engine**
(http://www.scottish.parliament.uk/search.html). Make sure that you click on the
box marked 'Written Questions/Answers'. This will limit your search only to that
database. For more detailed advice on how to use the Scottish Parliament web-site
search engine effectively, go the **Guide to Searching** page
(http://www.scottish.parliament.uk/help.htm).

▶   **National Statistics** (http://www.statistics.gov.uk/)

The **Bookshelf** (http://www.statistics.gov.uk/OnlineProducts/default.asp) section
of this web-site contains links to all products available in full-text, grouped by
theme. Many Scottish-specific publications can be found here, such as:

▶   **Scottish Abstract of Statistics** (http://www.scotland.gov.uk/library/sas/sa00-
00.htm)

▶   **Scottish Economic Statistics** (http://www.scotland.gov.uk/stats/ses2000/secs-00.asp)

▶   **Scottish Environment Statistics** (http://www.scotland.gov.uk/library/stat-ses/ses-
00.htm).

The **Bookshelf** section also contains links to important UK publications that contain
Scottish data:

▶   **New Earnings Survey** (http://www.statistics.gov.uk/nsbase/downloads/theme_
labour/NES00UK_1.pdf)

▶   **Regional Trends** (http://www.statistics.gov.uk/downloads/theme_compendia/
regional_trends/RT35_00_PRELIMS.pdf)

▶   **Social Trends** (http://www.statistics.gov.uk/nsbase/downloads/theme_social/
st30v8.pdf)

▶   **Neighbourhood Statistics** (http://www.statistics.gov.uk/neighbourhood/
home.asp) – this section of the web-site is an innovative long-term project to
make information widely available for thousands of small areas across the UK. It
will eventually offer users ready access to a vast range of social and economic
aggregate data based on a consistent small area geography. See the Data Catalogue
(http://www.statistics.gov.uk/neighbourhood/catalogue.asp) for details of what
data is presently available.

Economy

(http://www.scotland.gov.uk/stats/economy.htm)

▶   **Economy** (http://www.scotland.gov.uk/stats/stat-search.asp?pillar=economy&key= trad,taxa,logf,thec) - links to a number of key Scottish economic statistical publications and guides including:

▷   **Scottish Economic Statistics** (http://www.scotland.gov.uk/stats/ses2001/ ses-00.asp) - see above.

▷   **Scottish Economic Report** (http://www.scotland.gov.uk/library3/economics/ ser01-00.asp) – an electronic version of the twice yearly printed publication. It provides not only a comprehensive range of economic data but also commentary on the relevant data and sets the Scottish economy in a wider context.

The Scottish Executive Enterprise and Lifelong Learning Department has two very useful pages on its web-site for users of statistics. One is its **Publications** page (http://www.scotland.gov.uk/whatwedo.asp?type=pub&topic=enterprise), which provides links to all its publications, including statistical ones while the other is a **Statistics** page (http://www.scotland.gov.uk/who/elld/stats.asp) which provides links to the following datasets:

▷   **Scottish Production Database** (http://www.scotland.gov.uk/stats/spd/) - data on the production sector covering employment figures and financial details such as turnover, purchases, stocks and capital investment. Data can be classified according to industry group, geographical area and country of ownership.

▷   **Scottish Services Database** (http://www.scotland.gov.uk/stats/ssd/) - data on the service sector covering employment figures and financial details such as turnover, purchases, gross wages and salaries, and capital investment. Data can be classified according to industry group and geographical area.

▷   **Scottish Gross Domestic Product** (http://www.scotland.gov.uk/stats/bulletins/ 00077-00.asp) - estimates are available for all industries at a broad level and at a more detailed level, where possible. This is now being issued as a news release.

▷   **New Deal Statistics** (http://www.scotland.gov.uk/stats/bulletins/00078-00.asp) - a series of statistics relating to the New Deal programmes in Scotland for young people and the long-term unemployed.

▷   **Local Area Economic Profiles** (http://www.scotland.gov.uk/who/elld/stats_ LocalAuth0.asp) - key facts on the economy and labour market for each unitary authority area in Scotland, comparing each with the Scotland average.

Other useful web-sites containing data on the economy

▶ **Scottish Parliament** (http://www.scottish.parliament.uk/) includes **Sources of Statistics** on the Scottish Economy (http://www.scottish.parliament.uk/whats_happening/research/pdf_subj_maps/smda00-01.pdf) - see above.

▶ **Department of Trade and Industry** (http://www.dti.gov.uk/) which includes **Regional Competitiveness Indicators** (http://www.dti.gov.uk/sd/rci/) - bi-annual indicators providing 14 statistics which illustrate the factors determining the regional competitiveness of the English regions as well as of Scotland, Wales and Northern Ireland. Only the current edition is available on the web.

▶ **Commerce** (http://www.scotland.gov.uk/stats/stat-search.asp?pillar=economy&key=reta,ente) - the links are to publications and guides which are described under the general Economy heading and include:

▶ **Scottish Services Database** (http://www.scotland.gov.uk/stats/ssd/).

▶ **Scottish Gross Domestic Product** (http://www.scotland.gov.uk/stats/bulletins/00077-00.asp)

▶ **Scottish Economic Statistics** (http://www.scotland.gov.uk/stats/ses2001/ses-00.asp).

▶ **Energy and industry**
(http://www.scotland.gov.uk/stats/stat-search.asp?pillar=economy&key=busi,elec,gas,inte,manu,mini,nucl,oil,cons) - the links are to publications and guides which are described under the general Economy heading and include:

▶ **Scottish Production Database** (http://www.scotland.gov.uk/stats/spd/).

▶ **Scottish Services Database** (http://www.scotland.gov.uk/stats/ssd/).

▶ **Scottish Gross Domestic Product** (http://www.scotland.gov.uk/stats/bulletins/00077-00.asp)

▶ **Scottish Economic Statistics** (http://www.scotland.gov.uk/stats/ses2001/ses-00.asp).

Other useful web-sites containing commerce, energy and industry data

▶ **National Statistics** (http://www.statistics.gov.uk/) data on Commerce, Energy and Industry is best accessed through the Commerce (http://www.statistics.gov.uk/themes/commerce/default.asp) theme section of the web-site.

▶ **Department of Trade and Industry** (http://www.dti.gov.uk/) - national figures will again be found in many of the publications emanating from this department.

▶ **Labour market** (http://www.scotland.gov.uk/stats/stat-search.asp?pillar= economy&key=lama) - links to a number of key publications and guides on the labour market in Scotland including:

▶ **Scottish Economic Statistics** (http://www.scotland.gov.uk/stats/ses2001/ ses-00.asp) - chapter four of the current published edition particularly relates to the labour market.

▶ **Scottish Social Statistics** - The **Labour Market** section of the Scottish Social Statistics web-site (http://www.scotland.gov.uk/stats/sss/sss-04.asp) gives some interactive data. For the most detailed and fastest access to the data available, go directly to chapter 4 of the **pdf version** of the current published edition (http://www.scotland.gov.uk/stats/sss/docs/sss.pdf).

Other useful web-sites containing labour market data

▶ **Unemployment in Scotland** - a monthly publication produced by the Scottish Parliament Information Centre (SPICe) in a pdf format. This publication is only available electronically from the **Research Publications** (http://www.scottish. parliament.uk/whats_happening/research/subj_indx.htm) section of the Scottish Parliament web-site.

▶ **National Statistics** (http://www.statistics.gov.uk/) data on the labour market is best accessed through the Labour Market (http://www.statistics.gov.uk/ themes/labour_market/default.asp) theme section of the web-site.

| People |
(http://www.scotland.gov.uk/stats/people.htm)

▶ **Social and welfare** (http://www.scotland.gov.uk/stats/stat-search.asp?pillar= people&key=sose,soin) - the key publications on social and welfare statistics are:

▶ **Scottish Community Care Statistics** (http://www.scotland.gov.uk/stats/bulletins/ 00044-00.asp) – this annual publication brings together a wealth of information across the whole range of health and social care services for adults in Scotland. Also available in pdf format (http://www.scotland.gov.uk/stats/bulletins/ 00044.pdf).

▶ **Scottish Household Survey** web-site (http://www.scotland.gov.uk/shs/). This important survey of the people of Scotland is designed to provide up-to-date information about the characteristics, attitudes and behaviour of households and individuals on a range of issues, including principally local government, social justice and transport. The web-site provides access to the regular quarterly and annual reports arising from it:

▶ **Scotland's People: results from the Scottish Household Survey** (http://www.scotland.gov.uk/shs/docs/rep99-v1.pdf) – published annually, it provides detailed results from the Survey about people living in Scotland today. It covers such characteristics as household behaviour relating to transport, social inclusion and public services. It is supplemented by the quarterly **Scottish Household Survey Bulletin** (http://www.scotland.gov.uk/shs/docs/shsb-00.asp).

▶ **Scottish Social Statistics** (http://www.scotland.gov.uk/stats/sss/sss-00.asp) - contains a whole range of statistics on contemporary Scottish society. The Scottish Social Statistics web-site contains some interactive elements and it is intended that over time the web version will be added to, as more information becomes available. Also available in **pdf format** (http://www.scotland.gov.uk/stats/sss/docs/sss.pdf).

Other relevant publications from the Scottish Executive

▶ **Equality in Scotland: Guide to Data Sources** (http://www.scotland.gov.uk/stats/gtds-00.asp) - a valuable guide to the main sources of statistical information on equality issues in Scotland, which include the following titles:

▶ **Equality in Scotland - Disabled People** (http://www.scotland.gov.uk/library3/society/equality/esd-00.asp)

▶ **Equality in Scotland - Ethnic Minorities** (http://www.scotland.gov.uk/library3/society/equality/esem-00.asp)

▶ **Equality in Scotland - Older People** (http://www.scotland.gov.uk/library3/society/equality/esop-00.asp)

▶ **Equality in Scotland - Women and Men** (http://www.scotland.gov.uk/library3/society/equality/esmw-00.asp)

▶ **Men and women: a statistical profile** (http://www.scotland.gov.uk/stats/mnw-00.asp) - a valuable statistical source providing figures, disaggregated by gender, across a range of social and economic topics. Also available in **pdf format** (http://www.scotland.gov.uk/stats/mnw.pdf)

Other useful web-sites containing Social and Welfare data

▶ **National Statistics** (http://www.statistics.gov.uk/) - data on social and welfare matters is best accessed through the **Social and Welfare** (http://www.statistics.gov.uk/themes/social_finances/default.asp) theme section of the web-site.

▶ **Neighbourhood Statistics** http://www.statistics.gov.uk/neighbourhood/home.asp) - this section of the National Statistics web-site also contains a whole range of data for Scotland, at both Ward and Local Authority level, on social security benefits and deprivation indices. See the **Data Catalogue** (http://www.statistics.gov.uk/neighbourhood/catalogue.asp) for details.

▶ **Health and Care** (http://www.scotland.gov.uk/stats/stat-search.asp?pillar= people&key=heal,sowo,drmi) – lists the relevant Scottish Executive publications and sources. However, the best source for health statistics on the web is the **Information and Statistics Division of the NHS Scotland** (http://www.show.scot. nhs.uk/isd) site. Information is accessible in a number of ways :

▶ **Health Topic** (http://www.show.scot.nhs.uk/isd/health_topics/health_topics.htm) - this section contains a list of current health topics, arranged alphabetically or by key health topic area:

   ▶ **Cancer** (http://www.show.scot.nhs.uk/isd/cancer/cancer.htm), which includes **Cancer Facts and Figures** and **Selected Publications** containing cancer data.

   ▶ **Child Health** (http://www.show.scot.nhs.uk/isd/child_health/child_health.htm).

   ▶ **Coronary Heart Disease** (http://www.show.scot.nhs.uk/isd/heart_disease/heart_ disease.htm), which includes **Trends** (http://www.show.scot.nhs.uk/isd/heart_ disease/chd_trends/chd_trends.htm) and **Treatment figures** (http://www.show. scot.nhs.uk/isd/heart_disease/chd_treatments/chd_treatments.htm).

   ▶ **Mental Health** (http://www.show.scot.nhs.uk/isd/mental_health/mental_ health.htm).

   ▶ **Primary Care** (http://www.show.scot.nhs.uk/isd/primary_care/primary_ care.htm), which includes **General Medical Practice** (http://www.show.scot. nhs.uk/isd/primary_care/gmp/gmp.htm) / **Prescribing and Dispensing** (http://www.show.scot.nhs.uk/isd/primary_care/pservices/pcare_pservices.htm) / **Dental Services** (http://www.show.scot.nhs.uk/isd/primary_care/dental/ pcare_dental.htm) data.

   ▶ **Clinical Governance** (http://www.show.scot.nhs.uk/isd/clinical_gov/clinical_ gov.htm) which includes:

      ▶ **CRAG** (Clinical Resource and Audit Group) (http://www.show.scot.nhs.uk/crag/) Annual clinical outcome indicators – the latest report presents indicators in maternal health, child health and dental health in children. It also includes a major section exploring trends in emergency admissions to Scottish hospitals as well as a detailed section on colorectal cancer.

      ▶ **SHIP** (Summary Health Information Pages) (http://www.show.scot.nhs.uk/ isd/SHIP/home.htm)- high level basic summary health information from the late eighties through to the present day, for Scotland and individual Health Board areas, encompassed in four main modules - Activity, Primary Care, Waiting Times and Workforce. The data are presented in a series of Microsoft Excel workbooks and tables.

▶ **Publications** (http://www.show.scot.nhs.uk/isd/publications/publications.htm) - provides a listing of recent and forthcoming publications (arranged by date) which are hypertexted linked (if an electronic version is available). At the foot of the page there are alphabetical listings to all publications. Simply click on the appropriate icon to connect to the page. Important publications such as **Scottish Health Statistics 2000**, the **Scottish Health Survey 1998** and **Scottish Health Service Costs 2000** can be located from this site. It is important to note that many publications available on the ISD web-site are in acrobat format. You can download this software easily and free of charge from the **Adobe Acrobat** web-site (http://www.adobe.co.uk/products/acrobat/readstep.html).

▶ **Search** (http://www.show.scot.nhs.uk/isd/search.asp) - you can search either the entire ISD web-site or by particular health topic. A Quick Search option is also available on the navigation column on the left of the screen.

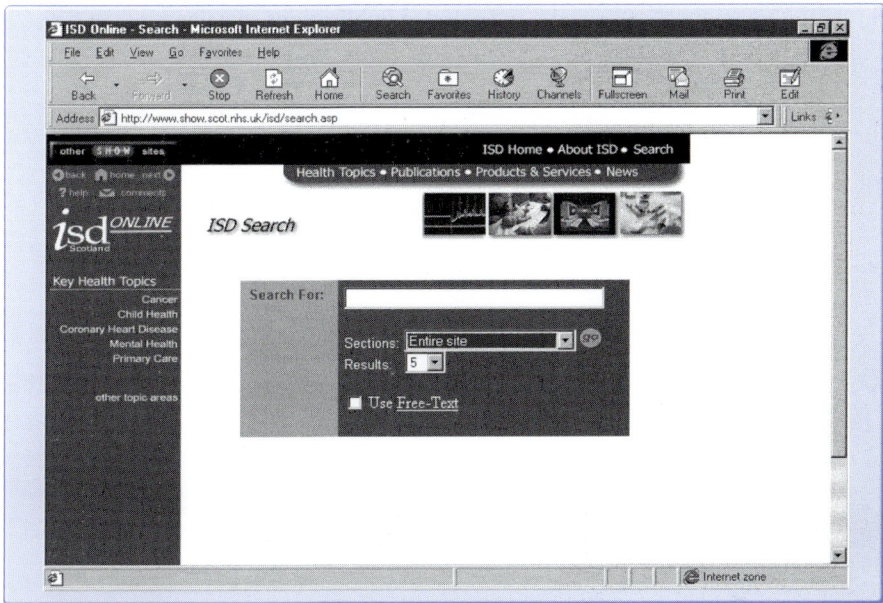

© Crown copyright

Other useful sites which contain health data

▶ **General Register Office for Scotland** (http://www.gro-scotland.gov.uk) for mortality statistics (See section on Population and Migration for more detailed information).

▶ **Health Education Board for Scotland** (http://www.hebs.scot.nhs.uk/) - the **Research Centre's Survey Data web-site** (http://www.hebs.scot.nhs.uk/researchcentre/sd/index.htm) contains links to the Health Education Population Survey and the Health Behaviours of School-Aged Children survey

▶ **Public Health Institute of Scotland** (http://www.show.scot.nhs.uk/phis/) - which hosts the **Constituency Health Reports** (http://www.show.scot.nhs.uk/phis/constituencyprofiles/national.htm) - contain data on healthcare and illness, prosperity and poverty, educational attainment and lifestyle behaviour.

▶ **Scottish Centre for Infection and Environmental Health -SCIEH online** (http://www.show.scot.nhs.uk/scieh/) which provides data on communicable diseases.

- **Scottish Social Statistics** (http://www.scotland.gov.uk/stats/sss/sss-00.asp) - the **Health and Care** section of the Scottish Social Statistics web-site (http://www.scotland.gov.uk/stats/sss/sss-06.asp) gives some interactive data. For the most detailed and fastest access to the data available go directly to chapter 6 of the **pdf version** of the current published edition (http://www.scotland.gov.uk/stats/sss/docs/sss.pdf).

- The **Department of Health's Statistics on the Web** (http://www.doh.gov.uk/public/stats3.htm) contains data that mostly relates to England and Wales. However, some UK or Great Britain level data that includes Scottish information is available.

- **National Statistics** (http://www.statistics.gov.uk/) - data on Health is best accessed through the **Health and Care** (http://www.statistics.gov.uk/themes/health_care/default.asp) theme section of the web-site.

- **World Health Organisation** (http://www.who.int/) - hosts a cancer database called **WHO Databank** (http://www-dep.iarc.fr/dataava/globocan/who.htm) which contains detailed cancer mortality data by year, by country and by cancer. Data is available for Scotland (under the heading United Kingdom, Scotland) from 1950 onwards.

- **Population and Migration** (http://www.scotland.gov.uk/stats/stat-search.asp?pillar=people&key=marr,immi,popu,etmi) – lists the relevant Scottish Executive publications and sources. However, the best source for statistics on population and migration on the web is the **General Register Office for Scotland** (http://www.gro-scotland.gov.uk), the department responsible for the registration of births, marriages, deaths, divorces and adoptions in Scotland, and for co-ordinating the decennial censuses of Scotland's population. A wealth of demographic data is accessible through the **On-Line Data Library** (http://www.gro-scotland.gov.uk/grosweb/grosweb.nsf/pages/library), which is arranged by four main topics:

- Population - annual, quarterly and estimated returns.

- Vital Events - births, deaths, marriages, divorces and adoptions.

- Miscellaneous Statistics - electoral statistics.

- General Information Interest - including most popular forenames and surnames.

Most of the data sources in the Population and Vital Events topics are taken from:

- **Annual Report of the Registrar-General for Scotland** (http://www.gro-scotland.gov.uk/grosweb/grosweb.nsf/pages/99annrep) - contains commentary and detailed tabular information on population, births, deaths, cause of death, stillbirths and infant deaths, marriages, divorces and other related topics.

- **Registrar General's Quarterly Return** (http://www.gro-scotland.gov.uk/grosweb/grosweb.nsf/pages/00quart4) - which contains provisional data on births, deaths, cause of death and marriages occurring in Scotland, much of which is broken down by sex, age and area.

▶ **Registrar General's Preliminary Return** (http://www.gro-scotland.gov.uk/ grosweb/grosweb.nsf/pages/00prelim) - a selection of tables giving provisional annual vital event data. This is generally issued in April of the following year and is superseded by the publication of the Annual Report in July.

▶ **Mid-year population estimates** (http://www.gro-scotland.gov.uk/grosweb/ grosweb.nsf/pages/myeh00) - produced annually, they relate to 30 June of the relevant year and are generally released during April of the following year.

▶ **Population projections** (http://www.gro-scotland.gov.uk/grosweb/grosweb.nsf/ pages/pp98) - prepared at regular intervals by the Government Actuary's Department in consultation with GRO(S). These projections are used as a basis for preparing **sub-national projections** (http://www.gro-scotland.gov.uk/ grosweb/grosweb.nsf/pages/98snpp) for the local authority and health board areas of Scotland. The intention is to publish future projections on a biennial basis, whenever possible.

Please note that most of the above tables are made available as 'Lotus 1-2-3 .wk1' spreadsheet files. When you 'click on the links', your browser, depending on how it has been configured, will prompt to either open the file or save it to disk.

▶ **Search** (http://www.gro-scotland.gov.uk/grosweb/grosweb.nsf/pages/search) - allows the user to search the entire GRO(S) site. It is possible to limit a search by number, relevance and date.

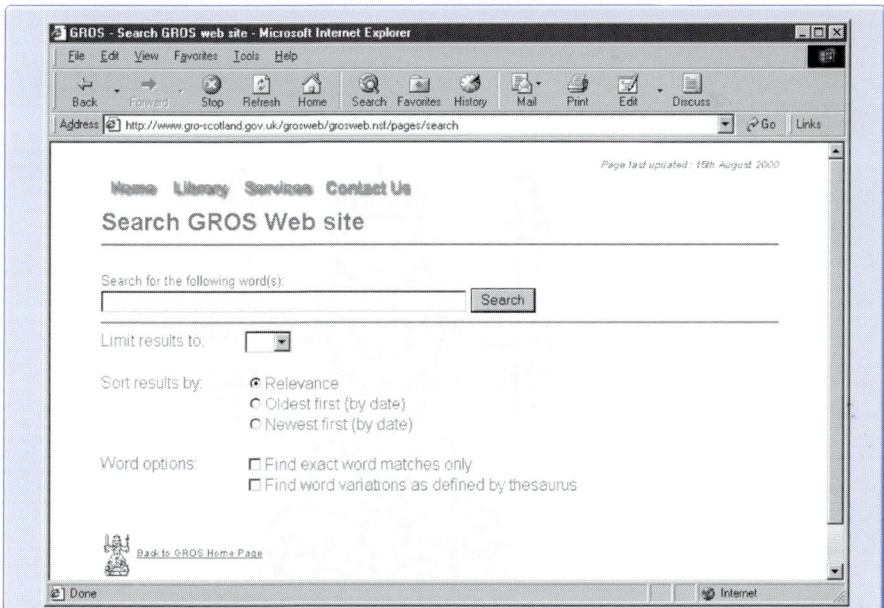

Other useful sites which contain population data

- ▶ **Scottish Social Statistics** (http://www.scotland.gov.uk/stats/sss/sss-00.asp) - the **Population, Households and Families** section of the Scottish Social Statistics web-site (http://www.scotland.gov.uk/stats/sss/sss-01.asp) gives some interactive data. For the most detailed and fastest access to the data available, go directly to chapter 1 of the **pdf version** of the current published edition (http://www.scotland.gov.uk/stats/sss/docs/sss.pdf).

- ▶ **National Statistics** (http://www.statistics.gov.uk/) - population and migration data is best accessed through the **Population and Migration** (http://www.statistics.gov.uk/themes/population/default.asp) theme section of the web-site.

- ▶ **Education and training** (http://www.scotland.gov.uk/stats/educ.htm) – Education statistics have increasingly moved from the publication of bulletins to shorter news releases with accompanying tables. From 2001, all new web documents will include both HTML (web-page) and downloadable PDF (acrobat) versions as a matter of course. There are four sub-headings to the Education and Training section – schools, further education, higher education, and general and training - but, given the inter-related nature of the 'post-school' statistics, the latter three will be considered together.

- ▶ **Schools** (http://www.scotland.gov.uk/stats/stat-search.asp?pillar=people&key=scho,pupi) – a wide range of statistics are produced on all aspects of schools, of which the five key publications, giving information at individual school level, by education authority and across Scotland as a whole, are:

  - ▶ **Attendance and Absence in Scottish Schools** (http://www.scotland.gov.uk/library3/education/aass-00.asp) – arranged by education authority and including grant-aided and self-governing schools.

  - ▶ **Budgeted School Running Costs** (http://www.scotland.gov.uk/stats/bulletins/00069-00.asp) - a new bulletin providing information formerly supplied by 'Scottish Schools: Costs' on running costs for primary and secondary schools.

  - ▶ **Destinations of Leavers from Scottish Schools** (http://www.scotland.gov.uk/stats/bulletins/00048-00.asp) - a new bulletin providing information about the destinations of leavers from Scottish schools, including independent and grant-aided schools. This was previously supplied in the report entitled 'Leaver Destinations from Scottish Secondary Schools'. The most recent issue covers the period 1997-98 to 1999-2000. Tables give information on schools by council.

  - ▶ **Examination Results in Scottish Schools** (http://www.scotland.gov.uk/library2/doc08/erss-00.htm) – covers results for Standard and Higher Grades, Certificate of Sixth Year Studies and National Certificate qualifications.

▶ **Summary Results of the [dated] School Census** (http://www.scotland.gov.uk/stats/bulletins/00013-00.asp) - provides figures for primary, secondary and special schools, and includes data on teacher numbers, class sizes and special needs.

▶ Further Education, Higher Education, General and Training

▶ **Higher Education Graduates and Diplomates and their First Destinations** – the most recent bulletin contains information on students, from both Higher Education Institutions and Further Education Colleges, who successfully completed a higher education course in Scotland. In particular, information is shown for the first destination of students after graduating. It replaces 'First Destination of Graduates and Diplomates'. This is now issued and updated by news releases.

▶ **Participation in Education by 16-21 Year Olds in Scotland** – the most recent bulletin was for the period, 1987-88 to 1997-98 and this is now updated by a news release.

▶ **Student Awards in Scotland** – now appearing as a news release containing information on the numbers of full time students on Higher Education courses who received awards through the Student Awards Agency for Scotland, and the costs of these awards.

▶ **Students in Higher Education in Scotland** – now updated by a news release that focuses on students in Higher Education Institutions (HEIs) and includes figures on graduate numbers.

Note that information about individual schools or further education institutions may also be found on the web-site of the relevant local authority.

Other useful sites which contain education data

▶ **Scottish Social Statistics** (http://www.scotland.gov.uk/stats/sss/sss-00.asp) is also a useful source of education data. The **Education** section of the Scottish Social Statistics web-site (http://www.scotland.gov.uk/stats/sss/sss-03.asp) gives some interactive data but for the most detailed and fastest access to the data available go directly to chapter 3 of the **pdf version** of the current published edition (http://www.scotland.gov.uk/stats/sss/docs/sss.pdf).

▶ **Scottish Further Education Funding Council** (http://www.sfefc.ac.uk) – statistical information on the 47 Further Education colleges in Scotland, including the INFACT database which provides figures on students and courses, in addition to in-year, bursary and enrolment statistics.

▶ **Scottish Higher Education Funding Council** (http://www.shefc.ac.uk/) also produces **statistical bulletins** (http://www.shefc.ac.uk/publicat/statistics/Publications/Pubsintro.htm), particularly in relation to students eligible for funding by subject group, level of degree and mode of study. SHEFC publishes a leaflet annually giving key tables on the amounts of recurrent funding allocated by the Council, the number of eligible students by subject group, recurrent income of institutions and other related statistics.

▶ **Department for Education and Skill Statistics** (http://www.dfes.gov.uk/ statistics/) web-site includes **Education and Training Statistics for the United Kingdom** (http://www.dfes.gov.uk/statistics/DB/VOL/v0211/index.htm). This is the primary source of education and training statistics for the UK as a whole, providing an integrated overview of statistics on education and training in the UK in over 50 tables. Many of the tables allow comparisons to be made over time and also between the four countries. Also available in **pdf format** (http://www.dfes.gov.uk/statistics/DB/VOL/v0211/vol05-2000.pdf).

▶ **National Statistics** (http://www.statistics.gov.uk/) - education data is best accessed through the **Education and training** (http://www.statistics.gov.uk/ themes/education/default.asp) theme section of the web-site.

▶ **Housing** (http://www.scotland.gov.uk/stats/stat-search.asp?pillar=people&key=hous)

▶ **Housing Trends in Scotland: Quarter Ending ...** - a statistical bulletin presenting standard quarterly analysis of housing activity in Scotland, including public sector house sales, new house building, homelessness applications and the improvement of existing dwellings. It also contains annual information on public sector stock and vacancy rates, the provision of housing for the elderly and disabled, local authority estimates of the number of Below Tolerable Standard dwellings, and estimates of stock by tenure. Most of the figures are collected and prepared by the Scottish Executive Housing Statistics Branch from local authorities, housing associations and Scottish Homes, unless otherwise stated. This is also available in pdf format.

▶ **Household Projections for Scotland** (http://www.scotland.gov.uk/stats/ bulletins/00019-01.asp) – a statistical bulletin presenting year-based household projections produced by the Scottish Executive Development Department. These are updated every two years and incorporate population projections as an indication of possible future trends.

▶ **Local Authority Housing Income and Expenditure** (http://www.scotland.gov.uk/ stats/bulletins/00028-00.asp) - provides factual information on local authority housing income and expenditure over the last three years.

▶ **Operation of the Homeless Persons Legislation in Scotland: National and Local Authority Analyses** (http://www.scotland.gov.uk/stats/bulletins/ 00018-00.asp) - a bulletin presenting statistics on applications made by households to Scottish local authorities for assistance under the homeless persons legislation during a ten-year period. The volume of applications, together with detailed analyses of how local authorities have assessed and dealt with cases, is provided at both national and local authority levels. This is now updated by a quarterly statistical release.

Other useful web-sites containing housing data

▶ **Scottish House Condition Survey** (http://www.scot-homes.gov.uk/research/cond96/) - a precis of the main findings showing the different categories covered by the survey.

▶ **Scottish Social Statistics** (http://www.scotland.gov.uk/stats/sss/sss-00.asp) is also a useful source of housing data. The Housing section of the Scottish Social Statistics web-site (http://www.scotland.gov.uk/stats/sss/sss-02.asp) gives some interactive data but for the most detailed and fastest access to the data available go directly to chapter 2 of the **pdf version** of the current published edition (http://www.scotland.gov.uk/stats/sss/docs/sss.pdf).

▶ **National Statistics** (http://www.statistics.gov.uk/) data on housing is best accessed through the **Natural and Built Environment** (http://www.statistics.gov.uk/themes/environment/default.asp) theme section of the web-site.

▶ **Housing Statistics** (http://www.housing.dtlr.gov.uk/research/hss/index.htm) pages on the **Department of Transport, Local Government and the Regions web-site** (http://www.dtlr.gov.uk/) contains data on all aspects of housing policy in Great Britain. The web-site is organised by 'sections' which are sign-posted from the homepage. Of particular interest is the publication **Housing Statistics** (http://www.housing.dtlr.gov.uk/research/hss/hs2000/index.htm) which is a compendium of statistics covering all aspects of housing in England. Where consistent data are available, tables also cover Great Britain and the United Kingdom. Note that tables can be viewed in either pdf or Excel formats.

State

(http://www.scotland.gov.uk/stats/state.htm)

▶ **Crime and justice** (http://www.scotland.gov.uk/stats/stat-search.asp?pillar=state&key=laor) - the bulk of the relevant statistics are produced by the Scottish Executive Justice Department. The key publications for this sector are, in alphabetical order:

▶ **Civil Judicial Statistics** (http://www.scotland.gov.uk/library3/justice/cjss-00.asp) - provides statistics relating to the business of the civil courts.

▶ **Costs, Sentencing Profiles and the Scottish Criminal Justice System** (http://www.scotland.gov.uk/library3/justice/s306-00.asp) - provides statistics on the costs of the criminal justice system and profiles of sentencing practice in the district and sheriff courts.

▶ **Criminal Proceedings in Scottish Courts** (http://www.scotland.gov.uk/stats/bulletins/00041-01.asp) - an annual bulletin that includes information on the types of crime or offence involved in court proceedings, sentencing outcomes and the characteristics of offenders. This is also available in **pdf format** (http://www.scotland.gov.uk/stats/bulletins/00041.pdf).

▶ **Homicides in Scotland** (http://www.scotland.gov.uk/library2/doc08/hsb98-00.htm) - this statistical bulletin, published every two years, provides statistics on crimes of homicide recorded by the police in Scotland in that year and the preceding decade. In every intervening year, a statistical news release is published which contains summary information.

▶ **Prison Statistics Scotland** (http://www.scotland.gov.uk/stats/bulletins/00040-00.asp) - an annual bulletin on the prison population.

▶ **Recorded Crime in Scotland** (http://www.scotland.gov.uk/stats/bulletins/00075-00.asp) - an annual bulletin that presents statistics on crimes and offences recorded and cleared up by the eight Scottish police forces.

Other useful web-sites containing Crime and Justice data

▶ **Scottish Executive's Central Research Unit** (http://www.scotland.gov.uk/cru/default.asp) - **Crime and Criminal Justice Research Programme's Research Findings and Research Publications** - a listing of all publications available on-line, including summaries of the results of the **Scottish Crime Surveys**.

▶ **Scottish Social Statistics** (http://www.scotland.gov.uk/stats/sss/sss-00.asp) is also a useful source of crime and justice data. The **Crime and Justice** section of the Scottish Social Statistics web-site (http://www.scotland.gov.uk/stats/sss/sss-07.asp) gives some interactive data. For the most detailed and fastest access to the data available go directly to chapter 7 of the **pdf version** of the current published edition (http://www.scotland.gov.uk/stats/sss/docs/sss.pdf).

▶ **National Statistics** (http://www.statistics.gov.uk/) data on Crime and Justice is best accessed through the **Crime and Justice** (http://www.statistics.gov.uk/themes/crime_justice/default.asp) theme section of the web-site.

▶ **Other government** (http://www.scotland.gov.uk/stats/stat-search.asp?pillar=state&key=gole)

▶ **Annual Expenditure Report** (http://www.scotland.gov.uk/library3/finance/aer-00.asp) - sets out how money has been spent in past years and how the Executive plans to spend it in the future. Also available in **pdf format** (http://www.scotland.gov.uk/library3/finance/aers.pdf).

▶ **Government Expenditure and Revenue in Scotland** (http://www.scotland.gov.uk/library3/government/gers-00.asp) - provides an analysis of the public finances in Scotland. Also available in **pdf format** (http://www.scotland.gov.uk/library3/government/gers.pdf).

- **Local Area Economic Profiles** (http://www.scotland.gov.uk/who/elld/stats_LocalAuth0.asp) - key facts on the economy and labour market for each unitary authority area in Scotland, comparing each with the Scotland average.
- **Scottish Economic Statistics** (http://www.scotland.gov.uk/stats/ses2001/ses-00.asp) - chapter 6, 'Other Aspects of Scotland's Economy' provides tables on government and local authority revenue and expenditure. Also available in **pdf format** (http://www.scotland.gov.uk/stats/ses2001/ses.pdf).
- **Scottish Local Government Financial Statistics** (http://www.scotland.gov.uk/library3/localgov/lgfs-00.asp) - an annual publication providing a series of tables relating to local authority accounts, including income and expenditure, outstanding debt, local taxes and local authority employment. Tables are also available in Excel format.

Other useful web-sites containing other government data

- **Electoral Statistics** (http://www.gro-scotland.gov.uk/grosweb/grosweb.nsf/pages/elstat01) - provides statistics about the number of electors by region, council area or constituency for the Scottish, Westminster and European Parliaments and local government.

Please note that these tables are made available as 'Lotus 1-2-3 .wk1' spreadsheet files. When you 'click on the links', your browser, depending on its configuration, will prompt to either open the file or save it to disk.

Land

(http://www.scotland.gov.uk/stats/land.htm)

- **Environment** (http://www.scotland.gov.uk/stats/stat-search.asp?pillar=land&key=enna,laus,rude,arre) - The major source of statistics on the environment in Scotland is:
- **Scottish Environment Statistics** (http://www.scotland.gov.uk/library/stat-ses/ses-00.htm) - an irregular publication which provides essential compilations of statistics on environmental topics such as land, atmosphere, water, conservation, radioactivity and recreation, again supported by maps, tables and charts.

Another relevant publication from the Scottish Executive is:
- **Scottish Vacant and Derelict Land Survey** (http://www.scotland.gov.uk/stats/bulletins/00066-00.asp) – an annual bulletin, which is the only national source for vacant and derelict land. This is also available in **pdf format** (http://www.scotland.gov.uk/stats/bulletins/00066.pdf).

The public body responsible for environmental protection in Scotland is the Scottish Environment Protection Agency (SEPA) (http://www.sepa.org.uk/) and it produces a range of reports, many of which include statistical material. Key titles with statistics from SEPA are:

- **Radioactivity in Food and the Environment** (http://www.sepa.org.uk/publications/environmental_reports/index.htm#rife) – an annual report on radiological surveillance programmes with many tables, graphs and maps.

- **Scottish Bathing Waters Report** (http://www.sepa.org.uk/publications/environmental_reports/index.htm#bw) – an annual report providing comprehensive information on Scotland's coastal and inland bathing waters, again with many graphs, charts and figures.

- **State of the Environment Reports** (http://www.sepa.org.uk/publications/environmental_reports/stateenv/soereport.htm) –first published in 1996 as an initial attempt to provide a national overview of Scotland's environment, this has subsequently been updated by a series of topic reports on:

  - **Improving Scotland's Water Environment (1999)** (http://www.sepa.org.uk/publications/environmental_reports/1996waterquality/report/text/watertext.htm),

  - **Air (2000)** (http://www.sepa.org.uk/publications/environmental_reports/air-report/index.htm) and

  - **Soil Quality (2001)** (http://www.sepa.org.uk/frontpage/soil_report.htm).

Other useful web-sites containing environmental data

- The **Environmental Protection Statistics** (http://www.defra.gov.uk/environment/statistics/index.htm) section of the **Department for Environment, Food and Rural Affairs** (http://www.defra.gov.uk/) web-site contains data on all aspects of environmental policy in Great Britain. The web-site is organised into sections that are sign-posted from the homepage. Of particular interest is the publication **Digest of Environmental Statistics** (http://www.defra.gov.uk/environment/des/index.htm) which is the reference document for environmental data, seen as a guide to assist informed policy and development both at home and in the international arena. Note that tables can be viewed in either pdf or Excel formats.

- **The UK National Air Quality Information Archive** (http://www.aeat.co.uk/netcen/airqual/welcome.html) - the definitive source for air pollution data and information in the UK.

- **National Statistics** (http://www.statistics.gov.uk/) - data on the Environment is best accessed through the **Natural and Built Environment** (http://www.statistics.gov.uk/themes/environment/default.asp) theme section of the web-site.

- **Transport, travel and tourism** (http://www.scotland.gov.uk/stats/stat-search.asp?pillar=land&key=aitr,rotr,ratr,tour,setr,tran) - the major source of statistics on transport in Scotland is:

- **Scottish Transport Statistics** (http://www.scotland.gov.uk/stats/bulletins/ 00021-00.asp) – an annual publication, providing summary information about all modes of transport, combined with trends over the past 10 years and some comparisons with figures for Great Britain (or the UK) as a whole. Topic specific chapters include road freight, toll bridges and road accidents. Main points summarise key statistics and bring out significant points.

Other significant titles include:

- **Bus and Coach Statistics** (http://www.scotland.gov.uk/stats/bulletins/ 00067-00.asp) - an annual bulletin based on figures provided by the Department of the Environment, Transport and the Regions. The tables compare statistics and trends for Scotland with the corresponding figures for Great Britain. The bulletin now provides statistics on the number of Public Service Vehicles with mechanisms that allow easy access for disabled or infirm persons. The bulletin is also available in **pdf format** (http://www.scotland.gov.uk/stats/bulletins/00067.pdf).
- **Household Transport: some Scottish Household Survey results** - a bulletin providing information from the Scottish Household Survey (SHS) about the transport facilities available to private households, and about some travel by household members. Further bulletins will provide information on such matters as the kinds of journeys made by adults, the variation in the patterns of transport and travel across Scotland, and year-to-year changes. This document is also available in pdf format.
- **Road Accidents Scotland** (http://www.scotland.gov.uk/library3/transport/ ras99-00.asp) - an annual publication presenting statistics, for the past year and earlier years, of the numbers of road accidents in which one or more people are injured or killed recorded by the police in Scotland. It has a commentary on the trends in accidents and casualties, more detailed analyses, comparisons with other countries, many charts and statistical tables, and a number of annexes, such as a calendar of events affecting road traffic, notes on the collection of statistics, and background information about the changes to the trunk road network. It is updated by:
- **Key Road Accident Statistics** (http://www.scotland.gov.uk/library2/doc16/ 99ras-00.asp) - a provisional annual bulletin presenting less detailed statistics on road accidents in Scotland extracted from the Road Accidents statistical database.

Other useful web-sites containing transport data

- **Transport Statistics** (http://www.transtat.dtlr.gov.uk/) pages on the **Department of Transport, Local Government and the Regions** (http://www.dtlr.gov.uk/) web-site contains data on all aspects of transport in Great Britain. The web-site is designed so that users can locate statistical information either by selecting publications produced by Transport Statistics, for example **Transport Statistics Great Britain** (http://www.transtat.dtlr.gov.uk/tables/tsgb00/text/tsgb.htm) or by the topical areas listed on the transport statistics homepage.

▶ **National Statistics** (http://www.statistics.gov.uk/) data on Transport is best accessed through the **Transport, Travel and Tourism** (http://www.statistics.gov.uk/themes/transport/default.asp) theme section of the web-site.

▶ **Agriculture, forests and fisheries** (http://www.scotland.gov.uk/stats/stat-search.asp?pillar=land&key=agff). The bulk of the relevant statistics are produced by the Scottish Executive Environment and Rural Affairs Department (SEERAD) which has a very useful **Publications page** (http://www.scotland.gov.uk/agri/) on its website, providing links to all their publications, including those containing statistics. The key publications for this sector are:

▶ **Agricultural Census** (http://www.scotland.gov.uk/agri/documents/agcen-jun00-00.asp) – this provides annual figures on such matters as land use, crops, livestock and labour. The detailed tables in 1999 (http://www.scotland.gov.uk/agri/documents/agcs-00.asp) showed the main topics by local authority area. The following year's final results gave figures for the years 1991 to 1999 for comparison.

▶ **Agricultural Facts and Figures** (http://www.scotland.gov.uk/agri/documents/afaf-00.asp) - provides summary indications concerning aggregate output, input, incomes and prices as well as results from the agricultural census and surveys.

▶ **Agricultural Sample Census - Final Results** (http://www.scotland.gov.uk/agri/documents/AC_1200-00.asp)- the results are produced from a sample of returns from about 10,000 main agricultural holdings (i.e. around one third of the total) and, as such, the estimates are subject to a degree of statistical uncertainty.

▶ **Economic Report on Scottish Agriculture** (http://www.scotland.gov.uk/agri/documents/ersa-00.asp) – a comprehensive consideration of the whole agricultural sector, combining information on output, input and income, finance, census results, and farm types and sizes.

▶ **Scottish Agriculture - Output, Input and Income Statistics** (http://www.scotland.gov.uk/agri/documents/ag_io_stats00-00.asp#summ) – provisional results based on the latest information available.

▶ **Scottish Sea Fisheries Statistics** (http://www.scotland.gov.uk/stats/bulletins/00022-00.asp)- records details of sea fish landings into Scotland and landings by Scottish based vessels abroad. Under devolution, a Scottish vessel is one, which is registered on the UK register of Seamen and Shipping at a Scottish port. Figures include details of vessels, landings (by species) and charts of the main quota areas.

Other useful web-sites containing agricultural data

▶ The **Statistics** page (http://www.defra.gov.uk/esg/default.htm) of the **Department for Environment, Food and Rural Affairs** (http://www.defra.gov.uk) web-site contains a wide range of figures on all aspects of farming and fishing in Great Britain. The Navigation bar on the left of the screen allows users to search the site by using the Index of Statistics (an alphabetical listing) or by going directly to the Publications section. Here users will find links to both the main compendia available, such as **Agriculture in the UK** (http://www.defra.gov.uk/esg/work_htm/ publications/cf/auk/current/auk_pdf.htm), as well as a range of more specialist items. Please note that documents are in Excel, Word and Portable Document Format.

▶ **National Statistics** (http://www.statistics.gov.uk/) data on Agriculture, Fisheries and Food is best accessed through the **Agriculture, Fisheries and Food** (http://www.statistics.gov.uk/themes/agriculture/default.asp) theme section of the web-site.

Glossary

Accompanying documents: Documents which must accompany a Bill on its introduction, explaining its provisions and the policy behind it, and stating whether it is within the Parliament's legislative competence.

Acts of the Scottish Parliament: The laws passed by the Parliament and receiving Royal Assent.

Advocate General for Scotland: The Scotland Office post which acts as the UK Government's Law Officer for Scottish matters, the Lord Advocate and Solicitor General for Scotland now being part of the Scottish Executive.

Audit Committee: A mandatory committee of the Parliament, with up to 11 members, which considers any accounts or documents laid before Parliament concerning matters relating to public expenditure and finance.

Auditor General for Scotland: An officer, nominated by the Parliament but appointed by the sovereign, who investigates financial control, accounting and audit, independently of both Parliament and the Executive.

Auditor General's report: One of the accompanying documents required for any Bill which will result in expenditure from the Scottish Consolidated Fund and which sets out the Auditor General's views on the appropriateness of such expenditure.

Bills: Draft laws during their parliamentary process, before becoming Acts of the Scottish Parliament.

Budget Bill: An Executive Bill authorising money to be paid out of the Scottish Consolidated Fund in a financial year, or to authorise money received in a financial year to be used without payment into the Fund. Such Bills are subject to special legislative processes.

Business Bulletin: An authoritative publication produced by the Parliament containing full details of current and future business, such as the business programme, the daily business list, written questions, and other matters to be notified to MSPs.

Business list: The Parliament agenda for each day it sits, listing the items to be considered and timings for the Parliament and its committees.

Cabinet: The group of senior ministers of the Scottish Government, comprising the First Minister, ministers and the Lord Advocate, but not the Solicitor General for Scotland.

Code of Conduct: A code of rules and guidance on standards of conduct by MSPs agreed by the Parliament, following a motion from the Standards Committee. At present, there has been no agreement on such a code.

Committee: A body of between five and 15 MSPs formed to deal with particular parliamentary business, such as inquiries into particular policies and actions of the Executive, and detailed scrutiny of Bills.

Competent matters: Matters within the remit of any particular parliamentary committee.

Consolidation Bill: A Bill to restate the law, possibly with amendments based on recommendations of the Law Commissions. Such Bills have a special form of legislative process.

Consultative Steering Group (CSG): The group set up by the Secretary of State for Scotland to consider the working of the Scottish Parliament and its infrastructure. Its membership included representatives of the main Scottish political parties and a wide range of civic and other interests. Its report, **Shaping Scotland's Parliament**, was published in January 1999.

Convener: The MSP who chairs a committee.

Council of the European Union: The main decision-making institution of the European Union. It is made up of Ministers from the 15 Member States with responsibility for the policy area under discussion at a given meeting (e.g. foreign affairs, agriculture, industry, transport).

Court of Justice and Court of the First Instance: Institution which ensures that European Community law is uniformly interpreted and effectively applied.

Court of Session: The supreme civil court in Scotland.

Daily Business List: The detailed programme of business for a particular day, with times when each item is to be taken, published in the Business Bulletin.

Debates: Proceedings in the Parliament involving discussion by MSPs on the motions before them.

Decision Time: The period, usually of no more than 30 minutes, at the end of a day's business in the Parliament (generally 5pm Monday-Thursday or 12 noon Friday) when decisions are taken on the questions before it.

Decisions: European Union legislation binding only on those to whom they are addressed. They are usually directed at a named Member State or organisation and require specific action.

Delegated legislation: Another term for subordinate legislation, i.e. that made by a minister or others using powers granted under primary legislation, such as an Act of the Scottish Parliament or UK Parliament.

Devolution: The process of decentralising the governance of Scotland, within the UK, from the central authorities (Westminster and Whitehall) to a Scottish

Parliament and Executive. Similar schemes have been implemented for Northern Ireland and for Wales.

Devolution issues: Legal questions as to the boundary between devolved matters and reserved matters, such as whether a power or action is within the competence of the Scottish Parliament, Scottish Ministers or Scottish Law Officers. These can be decided ultimately by the Judicial Committee of the Privy Council.

Devolved matters: Matters for which the Scottish Parliament and/or the Scottish Executive assume responsibility.

Directives: European Union legislation binding on all Member States but permit national governments to introduce their own legislation interpreting the Directive within a given time period.

Education, Culture and Sport Committee: A subject committee of the Parliament, with up to 11 members, which examines school and pre-school education, the arts, media and sport, and other matters within the responsibility of the Minister for Children and Education.

Emergency Bill: An Executive Bill which, if agreed to, is subject to a speedy legislative process. For example, all stages are taken in the Parliament rather than in committee, and the usual requirements for intervals between stages do not apply.

Enterprise and Lifelong Learning Committee: A subject committee of the Parliament, with up to 11 members, which deals with the Scottish economy, industry, tourism, training and further and higher education and other matters within the responsibility of the Minister for Enterprise and Lifelong Learning.

Equal Opportunities Committee: A mandatory committee of the Parliament, with up to 13 members, which deals with equal opportunities, and observance of equal opportunities within the Parliament.

European Commission: The executive body of the European Union responsible for implementing and managing policy.

European Committee: A mandatory committee of the Scottish Parliament, with up to 13 members, dealing with proposals for, and implementation of European legislation, and any European Union or European Community issue.

European Court of Human Rights: A multilateral judicial body established to ensure compliance with the Convention for the Protection of Human Rights and Fundamental Freedoms.

European Parliament: The legislative assembly of the European Union (EU).

Executive Bill: A Bill introduced into the Parliament by a member of the Scottish Executive. It must be accompanied by a statement from that Minister on its legislative competence, explanatory notes, and a policy memorandum.

Executive devolution: Powers granted to Scottish Ministers in areas which are reserved matters (i.e. where the Scottish Parliament does not have legislative power).

Explanatory notes: An 'accompanying document' to an Executive Bill which explains each provision of the Bill, and provides other information on its effects.

Finance Committee: A mandatory committee of the Parliament, with up to 11 members dealing with proposals and budgets for public expenditure, or for tax-varying resolutions, Budget Bills, and the handling of financial business.

Financial memorandum: An 'accompanying document' to a Bill setting out estimates of its administrative and other costs to the Scottish Administration, local authorities and others.

First Minister: The head of the devolved Scottish Executive.

General Register Office (Scotland): Office responsible for the registration of births, marriages, deaths, divorces and adoptions in Scotland, and for carrying out periodic censuses of Scotland's population.

Government: Used to describe the full ministerial team (i.e. members of the Scottish Executive plus junior Scottish Ministers).

Hansard: The official published reports of proceedings in the Westminster Parliament.

Health and Community Care Committee: A subject committee of the Parliament, with up to 11 members, concerned with health policy, the NHS in Scotland and other matters within the responsibility of the Minister for Health and Community Care.

High Court of Justiciary: The supreme criminal court in Scotland.

Holyrood: The proposed permanent location in Edinburgh of the new Scottish Parliament. Also used in the media to refer to the Scottish Parliament itself and the title of an informative magazine which provides current information on the Scottish Parliament.

Judicial Committee of the Privy Council: A court given an important statutory role in the resolution of legal issues under the devolution settlement, such as whether Bills passed by the Parliament are within the Parliament's legislative competence. It can also decide on other 'devolution issues'. Its decisions are binding on all other courts. The Judicial Committee for devolution purposes consists of Law Lords and others holding 'high judicial office', such as Court of Session judges.

Justice 1 and 2 Committees: Subject committees of the Parliament, with up to 11members, which examines matters relating to the administration of civil and criminal justice, the reform of the civil and criminal law and such other matters as fall within the responsibility of the Minister for Justice. These committees succeeded the Justice and Home Affairs Committee in January 2001.

Laid documents: The Parliament's Standing Orders provide rules as to the laying of relevant documents before the Parliament. Many such documents, (e.g. financial reports or annual reports of public bodies) are required to be published by the Parliament and treated in this way.

Law Officers: The senior legal advisers to the government. The two Scottish Law Officers, who are Scottish Ministers and members of The Scottish Executive, are the Lord Advocate and the Solicitor General for Scotland. Unlike other ministers, the Scottish Law Officers need not be MSPs. The UK Government's Scottish Law Officer is the new office of Advocate General for Scotland.

Lead committee: The parliamentary committee which takes the lead role in the relevant legislative process for a particular Bill or statutory instrument. Where such falls within the remit of more than one committee, the Parliament may decide which one to be the lead committee in that particular case.

Legislation: Primary laws enacted by the Parliament are known as Acts of the Scottish Parliament. Subordinate legislation (often also known as delegated or secondary legislation) can be made by Scottish and UK ministers or other public bodies, or by the monarch by Order in Council. Much subordinate legislation will be subject to scrutiny and/or approval by the Parliament and, frequently, by the UK Parliament.

Legislative competence: This is the key concept in the remit of the Parliament, as only legislation passed by the Parliament which is within its competence can be valid law. This area of competence is defined in various provisions of the Scotland Act 1998, generally in terms of what is to be regarded as outside the Parliament's competence, such as 'reserved matters' listed in schedule 5, or where incompatible with Convention rights or with Community law.

Local Government Committee: A subject committee, with up to 11 members, which examines matters relating to local government.

Lord Advocate: The senior Scottish Law Officer, and a member of The Scottish Executive and the Cabinet. Various protections exist in the devolution legislation for the independent position and role of the Lord Advocate, especially in connection with criminal prosecutions and the investigation of deaths.

Mandatory committee: A committee of the Scottish Parliament which standing orders require to be established. There are 8 such committees: Audit, Equal Opportunities, European, Finance, Procedures, Public Petitions, Subordinate Legislation and Standards.

Member's Bill: A public Bill, other than a committee Bill, introduced by an MSP who is not a member of the Scottish Executive (so that, for example, a junior Scottish Minister could introduce a member's Bill). Proposals for such Bills require the support of at least 11 other members within one month of notice of the proposal in order for the Bill to be introduced.

Member's business: Parliamentary proceedings where the business is initiated by a MSP who is not acting on the Executive's behalf, nor on that of any party or parliamentary committee. This could be a debate on a general issue, on a procedural matter or even proceedings on a member's Bill.

Minister: A politician who is a member of the government. The senior Scottish Government ministers are known as 'members of The Scottish Executive' or 'The Scottish Ministers', and most of them form the Scottish Cabinet. Junior Scottish Ministers, most of whom are deputy ministers, assist the members of the Scottish Executive. All ministers, other than the Scottish Law Officers, must also be MSPs and cannot also be at the same time ministers in the UK Government.

Minutes of Proceedings: These formally record all items of business and the results of any decisions, divisions and elections which took place.

Motion: A motion is a proposition or question considered and decided upon by the Parliament or a committee. Particular examples are business motions, procedural motions, motions of no confidence, tax-varying resolutions and motions of the First Minister.

Official Report: The Official Report is the authoritative report of proceedings (including committees and written answers) in the Scottish Parliament. It is 'substantially verbatim', which means that repetitions are omitted and obvious mistakes corrected while keeping to the issue of what is said.

Open Question Time: A period of up to 15 minutes each week immediately following Question Time (normally on a Thursday), when Open Questions to Ministers are taken.

Open Questions: Up to three questions to Ministers, selected by the Presiding Officer from among all oral questions submitted within the required period, to be answered at an Open Question Time.

Oral Question: A parliamentary question which requests an oral answer by a Minister either at Question Time or Open Question Time.

Parliament: From a Scottish perspective, the UK Parliament is generally referred to as 'Parliament' and the Scottish Parliament as 'the Parliament'.

Parliamentary Bureau: The body which arranges the business of the Parliament and its committees. It consists of the Presiding Officer, a representative of each party having more than five members, and a representative of any group from parties having fewer than five members.

Parliamentary week: The normal Parliamentary week is between the hours of 14.30 and 17.30 on Monday, 09.30 and 17.30 on Tuesday, Wednesday and Thursday and 09.30 and 12.30 on Friday. Generally, the Parliament can meet on any sitting day during these periods.

Petitions: A means through which members of the public can make representations to the Parliament for its consideration.

Plenary: The term to describe a meeting of the full Parliament

Policy Memorandum: A document which must accompany an Executive Bill setting out its policy objectives, any consideration of alternatives, consultations undertaken, and assessment of the effects of the Bill on equal opportunities, human rights, and other matters considered relevant by Ministers.

Presiding Officer: The person who, with two deputies, presides over meetings of the Parliament, and has a number of other important functions. The Presiding Officer, who is an MSP, is elected by the Parliament at its first meeting following a general election, or if there is a vacancy.

Primary legislation: Statutes enacted by a parliament, such as Acts of the UK Parliament, and Acts of the Scottish Parliament and, infrequently, Prerogative Orders in Council.

Private Bill: A Bill introduced by a person or body ('promoter') to obtain particular powers or benefits which may be in conflict with the general law, including a Bill relating the personal affairs or circumstances of the promoter. A Private Bill Committee is normally established for the duration of each Private Bill.

Privy Council: A body which once exercised much of the executive power of the monarch, and whose residual functions include the making of Orders in Council, aspects of the regulation of certain professions and universities, and the granting of royal charters. For devolution purposes, the Privy Council's Judicial Committee has an important role as a court in adjudicating on devolution issues.

Procedures Committee: A mandatory committee of the Parliament, with up to 7 members, to consider the practice and procedures of the business of the Scottish Parliament.

Promoter: The individual person, body or association of persons introducing a private Bill.

Public Bill: A Bill which is not a private Bill.

Public Petitions Committee: A mandatory committee of the Parliament, with up to 7 members, to consider and report on the admissibility of a public petition and what action to be taken on it.

Queen's Printer for Scotland: The office created by the Scotland Act 1998 to carry out certain printing and other functions (such as Crown copyright) in relation to Scottish Acts, subordinate legislation and other official material.

Question Time: A period of up to 30 minutes each week (normally on a Thursday) immediately before Open Question Time, when oral questions to ministers are taken.

Questions: A means by which MSPs can seek information or explanation from ministers (and the Presiding Officer). Questions can be for oral or written answer, and are governed by Standing Orders and detailed guidance from the Chamber Office.

Recommendations: European Union legislation not binding but outlining the opinions or position of the Community institutions on a topic. They are used mainly to promote the moral and political positions of the institutions.

Regulations: European Union legislation binding on all Member States and are directly applicable. Regulations do not require any additional action on the part of national governments and override any national legislation with which they might conflict.

Reporter: A member of a parliamentary committee appointed by it to report back on any competent matter.

Reserved matter: Matters which are reserved to the UK Parliament at Westminster and are therefore not within the legislative competence of the Scottish Parliament. The reserved matters are listed in schedule 5 of the Scotland Act 1998.

Resolution: The form by which decisions of the Parliament are taken. Resolutions do not have the force of law, but are effective as an expression of the will of the Parliament for internal parliamentary purposes.

Royal Assent: The stage in the legislative process when the approval of the Sovereign turns a Bill into an Act.

Rural Development Committee: A subject committee of the Parliament, of up to 11 members, which examines matters relating to rural development, agriculture and fisheries and other matters within the responsibility of the Minister for Rural Affairs. In January 2001 it changed its title from the Rural Affairs Committee.

Scotland Act 1998: The main legislation of the UK Parliament giving effect to the Government's devolution policy, passed 19 November 1998 (1998 Chapter 46).

Scottish Administration: Official umbrella term for the Scottish Executive, junior Scottish Ministers, certain non-Ministerial officers, and their staff.

Scottish Affairs Select Committee: A select committee of the House of Commons, consisting of 11 MPs, with a remit to examine the expenditure, administration and policy of the Scotland Office and of the Advocate General.

Scottish Consolidated Fund: The fund created by the Scotland Act 1998 into which payments are made by the Secretary of State or sums received by the Scottish Government, and out of which the spending of the Scottish Government comes.

Scottish Constitutional Convention: Body composed of a number of Scottish political parties and other public groups which produced the detailed proposals for a devolution scheme which contributed to the UK Government's policy.

Scottish Executive: The Scottish Executive is the statutory name for the group of senior Ministers of the Scottish Government, comprising the First Minister, other Ministers (except Junior Scottish Ministers), and the two Law Officers. With the exception of the Solicitor General, are all currently members of the Scottish Cabinet. 'The Scottish Executive' is also used for the Scottish Administration, the overall devolved Scottish Government.

Scottish Grand Committee: A standing committee of the House of Commons, consisting of all MPs for Scottish seats, with a range of functions under standing orders, from holding ministers to account through questions and debates to scrutiny of certain types of Scottish legislation. The existence and role of the committee is currently under review.

Scottish Office: The name of the department of the UK Government, under the Secretary of State for Scotland, which dealt with many areas of Scottish Government prior to the establishment of devolution. Though much of its work moved into the devolved Scottish Executive, there is still a government department in Whitehall responsible for Scottish matters – now the Scotland Office.

Scottish Parliament Information Centre (SPICe): The office of the Scottish Parliament, within the Communications Directorate, providing research and information services to the Parliament, its committees, MSPs and their staff.

Scottish Parliamentary Corporate Body: The statutory body which arranges the provision of staff, property and services for the Parliament. It comprises the Presiding Officer and four MSPs.

Secondary legislation: Legislation made by a minister or other person or body under powers granted in an Act (of either the UK or Scottish Parliament). Such legislation is usually in the form of Rules, Regulations or Orders, and made by Statutory Instrument.

Secretary of State for Scotland: The senior minister of the UK government dealing with Scottish affairs. Prior to devolution, the Secretary of State was the political head of The Scottish Office, and is now head of the Scotland Office. The Secretary of State for Scotland has, since the 1920s, been a member of the UK Cabinet.

Section: A part of the main body of an Act of the Scottish Parliament. Also, the name for the equivalent provision of a Bill. For Westminster Bills, this is known as a 'clause'.

Session: The period from the date of first meeting of the Parliament following a general election until it is dissolved. This period is four years, unless the Parliament is dissolved early. Note that a session of the UK Parliament is usually of approximately a year's duration and that the Westminster equivalent of a Scottish Parliament session is usually described as 'a parliament' (a period of a maximum of five years).

Sheriff Court: The lower court in Scotland which has both civil and criminal jurisdictions.

Sitting day: Under Standing Orders, a day when the Office of the Clerk is open, but not when the Parliament is in recess or dissolved. Meetings of the Parliament normally take place on a sitting day during the normal parliamentary week. Committee meetings are not restricted to sitting days.

Social Justice Committee: A subject committee of the Parliament, with up to 11 members, to examine matters relating to housing and the voluntary sector and other matters within the responsibility of the Minister for Communities other than local government. In January 2001, it changed its title from the Social Inclusion, Housing and Voluntary Sector Committee.

Stages of Bills: The various formal stages of consideration of a Bill by the Parliament. Stage 1 is a consideration of, and a decision on, a Bill's general principles. Stage 2 is a consideration of the details of a Bill by a parliamentary committee (or committees) or in Committee of the Whole Parliament. Stage 3 is a final consideration of a Bill and a decision whether it should be passed or rejected. Reconsideration is a further stage after a Bill has been passed if it has been subject to intervention by the Secretary of State for Scotland or certain law officers preventing it from going for Royal Assent.

Standards Committee: A mandatory committee of the parliament, of up to 7 members, which examines members' conduct and interests, and the adoption of any Code of Conduct for members. It has power to recommend that a member's rights and privileges be withdrawn.

Standing Orders: The rules of procedure governing the internal operation of the Parliament and its proceedings.

Subject committee: A committee, other than a mandatory committee, established by the Parliament to deal with a particular subject.

Subordinate legislation: An alternative term for delegated legislation, i.e. legislation made by a minister or others using powers granted under primary legislation, such as an Act of the Scottish or UK Parliaments.

Subordinate Legislation Committee: A mandatory committee of the Parliament, of up to 7 members, which examines subordinate legislation laid before the Parliament, and powers, generally or in particular legislation, to make subordinate legislation.

Transport and the Environment Committee: A subject committee of the Parliament of up to 11 members, to consider and report on transport, the environment and natural heritage and other matters within the responsibility of the Minister for Transport and the Environment.

Westminster: The popular name for the UK Parliament.

Whitehall: The popular name for the UK government generally, and the civil service bureaucracy in particular.

Witness: A person invited or required to attend the proceedings of the Parliament, or its committees for the purpose of giving evidence.

Written Question: A question lodged by a member which is either specified as being for written answer by a minister or the Presiding Officer, or is selected for oral answer at Question Time or Open Question Time, but has not been answered orally.

Index

References to the Glossary are in italics.

SFEFC *see* Scottish Further Education
   Funding Council
SHEFC *see* Scottish Higher Education
   Funding Council
SJ *see* Social Justice Committee
SL *see* Subordinate Legislation Committee
SLOGIN see Scottish Local Government
   Information Network
SPICe *see* Scottish Parliament Information
   Centre
SQA *see* Scottish Qualifications Authority
SSIs *see* Scottish Statutory Instruments
ST *see* Standards Committee
STRSN see Teacher Researcher Support
   Network
schools *see* education
Scotland Act 1998 53, *159*
Scotland Europa 90, 91, 115
Scotland Europa Papers 91
Scotland Forum 51-52
Scotland in Europe 90
Scotland Office 83-84
Scotland Research and Innovation 115
Scotland's People: results from the Scottish
   Household Survey 125, 137
Scotlis 114
Scots Origins 110
Scottish Abstract of Statistics 124, 126, 133
Scottish Administration *159*
Scottish Affairs Select Committee 80, *159*
Scottish Agricultural Science Agency (SASA)
   115
Scottish Agriculture - Output, Input and
   Income Statistics 150
Scottish Archive Network (SCAN) 115-116
Scottish Arts Council (SAC) 116
Scottish Bathing Waters Report 128, 148
Scottish CCC *see* Scottish Consultative
   Council on the Curriculum
Scottish Centre for Infection and
   Environmental Health (SCIEH) 128, 139
Scottish Charity Law Review Commission 49
Scottish Community Care Statistics 125, 136

Scottish Conservative and Unionist Party 120
Scottish Consolidated Fund *159*
Scottish Constitutional Convention *159*
Scottish Consultative Council on the
   Curriculum (Scottish CCC) 112
Scottish Convention Bureau 120
Scottish Council for Research in Education
   (SCRE) 116
Scottish Council for Voluntary Organisations
   116
Scottish Courts Group, The 54-57
Scottish Courts Service, The 54-57, 116
Scottish Courts web-site 55-56
Scottish Crime Survey (SCS) 125, 146
Scottish Criminal Cases Review Commission
   62, 117
Scottish Crop Research Institute 117
Scottish Cultural Resources Access Network
   (SCRAN) 117
Scottish Economic Bulletin 124, 126
Scottish Economic Report 124, 134
Scottish Economic Statistics 124, 132, 136, 147
Scottish Enterprise 117
Scottish Environment Statistics 125, 147
Scottish Environmental Protection Agency
   (SEPA) 117-118, 128-129, 148
Scottish European Resources Network
   (SERN) 91-92
Scottish Executive *159*
   Agencies 39
   annual expenditure statistics 125, 146
   departments *see below* (under individual
      names)
   organisation 38
   publications 123-126, 131-132
      format 38-39
      Papers 39-43
      subject areas
         agriculture 150
         care services 138
         commerce 135
         crime 54, 145-146
         economy 134, 135

Y